FAMOUS AMERICAN ILLUSTRATORS

FAMOUS AMERICAN ILLUSTRATORS

ARPI ERMOYAN

Quantum
Books

A C K N O W L E D G M E N T S

The Society of Illustrators wishes to express its thanks to all those whose cooperation and efforts made this book possible. We are especially grateful to the following individuals who so generously supplied us with photographs and credits of the artists' works: Walt and Roger Reed, Illustration House; Judy Goffman, American Illustrators Gallery; Alan Goffman; Charles Martignette; Kendra Krienke and Alan Daniel; Jack Potter; A. Emmet Stephenson, Jr.; Richard Marschall; Tony D'Amico; Janet and Arthur Weithas; Joan Anton; Margo Feiden; Everett Raymond Kinstler; Mr. and Mrs. Robert Crozier; Donald R. Johnson; Harvey Kahn; Mrs. William A. Smith; Mrs. Emily Filley; Abe Echevarria; Don Barron, Art Direction Book Company; Leslie Cabarga; Jean Hunnicutt; Tom Rockwell; and Hy Steirman, Hastings House.

For their cooperation we are also greatly indebted to the following museums and organizations: Linda Szekely, The Norman Rockwell Museum at Stockbridge; Vicki Pointer, Brandywine River Museum; Liz Dickinson, Delaware Art Museum; James A. Michener Museum; National Geographic Society; The National Portrait Gallery; The Greenwich Workshop; Schoonover Studios, Ltd.; Matthew Verze, Detroit Athletic Club; Carol Rosenberg, Lotos Club; The American Red Cross; NASA/Johnson Space Center; The Challenger for Space Education; Broadway National Bank; Motorola Corporation; National Parks Service; A.J. Fine Arts Ltd. & Sevenarts Ltd.; Roberta Miller Associates; and Fashion Institute of Technology.

Special thanks must go to Walt Reed of Illustration House, whose selfless assistance provided us with images from his great collection of art, and information from his vast knowledge of illustration.

Bernadette Evangelist, the designer of this book, will be rewarded in heaven for her patience in making type and image changes, for her great attention to detail and most certainly her talent and good taste in laying out all the pages.

We are greatly indebted to Janet Weithas for her relentless pursuit of credits and pictorial material from collectors and museums, and for her diligent research of art from the Society's Permanent Collection.

Terrence Brown, Director of the Society of Illustrators, lent the support needed to get this project underway, and without the vision and financial backing of publisher Brian Morris of Rotovision, this manuscript might still be looking for a home.

Arpi Ermoyan, former Director of the Society of Illustrators, rates a very special vote of thanks for creating a superb manuscript for this book. In addition to the endless hours spent researching and writing the biographies, a further round of applause is due her for the additional hours she spent shepherding every aspect of the production of this book.

We salute Gerald McConnell, the Society's Publications Chairman and mastermind behind *Famous American Illustrators*. He envisioned this project, volunteered his services and brought it to fruition, nurturing it every step along the way. His dedication to this project was purely a labor of love for illustration and for the Society of Illustrators itself.

CONTENTS

Artists appear according to the year of their induction into the Society of Illustrators Hall of Fame.

In 1894 Frederic Remington wrote a fan letter to Howard Pyle. He had just seen a reproduction of Pyle's latest illustration of an executed pirate sprawled on the sand, painted as an illustration for an article, "Sea Robbers of New York" by Thomas Janvier, with the title "Pirates used to do that to their captains now and then." Remington was fascinated by it and suggested an exchange of the original for one of his own—to be painted for Pyle. Upon receipt of the picture, he again wrote, "I

HOWARD PYLE*

have the defunct pirate, and it goes right up in my collection. It is simply all fired satisfying and all I am going to do is say 'much obliged' and 'it is one on me.' The 'Puncher' will gallop into Wilmington some day—a 'Puncher for your Pirate.' That's fair trade if I paint it well enough. I have so long wanted to own one of your pictures."**

FREDERIC REMINGTON

This incident occurred before the founding of the Society of Illustrators in 1901, but it is representative of the many such expressions of admiration for outstanding work done and similar informal exchanges made between illustrators before and since. This admiration is at the central idea of the establishment of the Hall of Fame in 1958 in a desire to honor the best work done in the profession on a more formal basis. In making annual selections from

living illustrators the need to add those great deceased artists who had come before soon became apparent.

The artists included in this book thus represent a double-distilled selection, passing both the test of time and the approbation of the members of the profession. And in a larger sense, the artists have also recorded their times; their work provides a history of nearly a century going back to the beginnings of the invention of halftone printing.

CHARLES DANA GIBSON

Several fortuitous events converged in the 1880s to launch a "Golden Age" of American Illustration. Recovery from the Civil War and expansion into the West had created a burgeoning economy. Major advances in printing technology were developed in the form of high-speed presses and binding techniques, as well as the invention of halftone plate making which, if crude at first, made it finally possible to reproduce the artists' works with greater fidelity to the original and at a much lower cost. National magazines provided cultural links to all parts of the country and their distribution was financially encouraged by Congress through postal subsidies for their educational value. In short, the country was prosperous, circulations of the magazines were increasing from month to month with new publications emerging to compete with the older ones; prosperous magazines could afford the best talents and paid higher fees to the writers and artists who illustrated them.

HARRISON FISHER

Artists responded with great enthusiasm to this national showcase for their pictures. The better illustrators had more work offered to them than they could handle, opening up opportunities

COLES PHILLIPS

for new talents. Full-color printing soon became possible. Through their appearances accompanying fiction within and covers on the outside, magazine illustrators became celebrities with coteries of fans and followers. Publishers quickly learned that a pretty girl on the cover sold more issues on the newsstand than one simply listing the table of contents. Charles Dana Gibson's girls became celebrities, inspiring a generation of young women to emulate them. They were soon joined by Howard Chandler Christy's girls, and those of Harrison Fisher and James Montgomery Flagg. Coles Phillips' "Fadeaway Girl" graced the covers of *Life* and also boosted newsstand sales whenever she appeared.

Other artists had their specialities as well. Frederic Remington was as famous as the Indians, cowboys and troopers he painted and was a personal friend of President Theodore

A. B. FROST

Roosevelt's whose stories he had earlier illustrated in *The Century* magazine. Howard Pyle had illustrated President Woodrow Wilson's five-volume *History of the American People* and was best known for his colorful paintings of Pirates and Buccaneers. Arthur Burdett Frost brought Joel Chandler Harris's "Uncle Remus" stories to visual life and was well known to sportsmen who admired the authenticity of his

ROSE O'NEILL

pictures of fishing, hunting, cycling and golfing.

*"Pirates used to do that to their Captains now and then," by Howard Pyle. Private Collection.
**From Charles D. Abbott, *Howard Pyle, A Chronicle*, New York, Harper & Bros. © 1925.

JESSIE WILLCOX SMITH

Illustration was also one of the earlier professions open to women, and their expertise in depicting mothers, children and social subjects found them a large appreciative audience in the family magazines. Among the most successful females were Elizabeth Shippen Greene, Jessie Willcox Smith, Alice Barber Stevens, Sarah Stillwell Weber, Violet Oakley, Rose O'Neill and Neysa McMein. (Many of them had been students of Howard Pyle's.)

Howard Pyle must be singled out for his great contributions to illustration, not only as one of the dominant talents of his era, but also as the most influential teacher of illustration in America. His select band of students, which included N.C. Wyeth, Harvey Dunn, Frank Schoonover and Stanley Arthurs, as well as most of the above-listed women, went on to major careers and, in turn, they taught the Pyle traditions to a third generation of outstanding illustrators including Dean Cornwell, Harold Von Schmidt and Saul Tepper. That line has continued, in various manifestations to the present, and Pyle rightfully wears the august mantle of "Father of American Illustration."

NEYSA McMEIN

From early on, despite their popular acceptance, illustrators were conversely ignored or dismissed by art critics. Although it is difficult to find many major American artists who did not

DEAN CORNWELL

do illustrations at some time in their careers, it was considered somehow more "commercial" to receive a fee from a magazine editor than from a private collector. True, an illustrator had to work within the constraints of a manuscript and not all writing would permit a lofty interpretation. However, many of the authors were important, among them Mark Twain, Ambrose Bierce, Willa Cather, William Faulkner, F. Scott Fitzgerald, Ernest Hemingway and Edna Ferber, and the illustrators were able to match them with important pictorial interpretations. Not that all the fiction had to be great literature—the best illustrators could find a worthy picture theme in even a vapid narrative.

Advertising presented a greater challenge, but artists such as Walter Biggs, Franklin Booth and Frederic Gruger managed to

WALTER BIGGS

make their pictures effective for their clients, as well as important works of art.

As time has passed, some of the prejudices against illustration have begun to fall away and a reappraisal of earlier illustrations has brought a recognition of the inherent quality in many of the drawings and paintings that had previously been snubbed. More illustrators are now included in museum collections or even have museums built around them, i.e. Norman Rockwell, Howard Pyle, N.C. Wyeth, Frederic Remington, Charles Russell, John Clymer and Harvey Dunn. Books are devoted to many illustrators including these as well as John Held Jr., A.B. Frost, Joseph Clement Coll, Coles Phillips, J.C. Leyendecker, Dean Cornwell, Harold Von Schmidt, James Montgomery Flagg, Donald Teague, Tom Lovell and many others. Private collectors have avidly sought their works and prices for originals by Rockwell, Maxfield Parrish or N.C. Wyeth can match those of many of the more mainstream American painters.

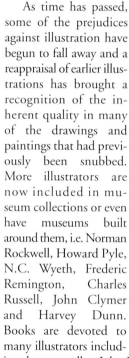

NORMAN ROCKWELL

Increasingly, as the art world goes into the age of the computer-generated image, the "made by hand" art will also be more appreciated for its technical skill. Hopefully, the future generation of illustrators will use the computer as but a new medium or tool for expression rather than as a recycler of stock images or graphic tricks. The potential is here for a rich creative future, but it will still need the traditional basic structures of form and content. There is no better yardstick than to look back at the talented and dedicated artists preceding them who have proudly called themselves illustrators and have contributed so much to America's art.

"While it may not be as well known as Cooperstown's Hall, the Illustrators Hall of Fame is no less the best of the best from a different field of dreams." So wrote Zoltan Bedy in an article describing the Society of Illustrators Hall of Fame exhibition at the Lowe Gallery at Syracuse University in February 1997.

The Hall of Fame was formed in 1958 with Society of Illustrators member Willis Pyle as its founding father and committee chairman, a position he held with distinction for the next 36 years. The premise of the Society of Illustrators Hall of Fame is as simple as its counterpart in Cooperstown—to induct and enshrine the superstars in its own field.

Once each year the Hall of Fame Committee, which is comprised exclusively of Society of Illustrators past presidents, meets to elect the new inductees. How wonderfully appropriate that in 1958, the first illustrator to be awarded that honor was Norman Rockwell, unquestionably the single most influential and beloved illustrator whose work ever graced the printed page.

Subsequent inductees were Winslow Homer, a brilliant illustrator/journalist during the Civil War; Charles Dana Gibson, the creator of that immortal icon, the Gibson Girl; J.C. Leyendecker, whose Arrow Collar man was the perfect visual equivalent of F. Scott Fitzgerald's Gatsby; James Montgomery Flagg, whose WWI Uncle Sam recruiting poster helped galvanize a nation much as Norman Rockwell's Four Freedoms did a quarter of a century later; and Rube Goldberg, the creator of those wonderfully wacky inventions, whose name became synonymous with technological overkill.

These illustrators, just a sampling from a roster that includes eighty-seven artists, have captured in paint, pencil and pen, the dreams, aspirations, hopes and fears of a public with their enormous skill, passion and imagination.

Artists are by nature iconoclasts, often opinionated and rarely, if ever, given to unanimous agreement. There is, however, a remarkable similarity in their response to learning that they have been elected to the Society of Illustrators Hall of Fame.

In 1992, Joe Bowler, whose magnificent editorial illustrations appeared regularly in virtually every major magazine for four decades, said "What an honor! What a surprise! My next reaction was a mental flow of all the great names included in the Illustrators Hall of Fame and I was very moved. To be given such an honor by your peers during your lifetime is truly a superb gift."

In 1995, James Avati, the creator of landmark paperback cover paintings that were to define that genre in the 1940s and 1950s, wrote "I am very much touched that I am considered worthy of this honor by my peers."

Rudyard Kipling once described journalism as "literature in a hurry." I sincerely believe this book offers ample evidence that illustration is "fine art on a deadline."

NORMAN ROCKWELL

WINSLOW HOMER

CHARLES DANA GIBSON

J. C. LEYENDECKER

JOE BOWLER

JAMES AVATI

I WANT YOU
FOR U.S. ARMY
NEAREST RECRUITING STATION

JAMES MONTGOMERY FLAGG

RUBE GOLDBERG

It was love at first sight between Norman Rockwell and *The Saturday Evening Post*, a relationship that flourished for over 40 years. After illustrating for *Boys' Life* magazine in his teens, at age 21 Rockwell took courage in hand and went to see the art director of the *Post*, who bought two illustrations on the spot and commissioned three more. Rockwell's first cover appeared on the May 20, 1916, issue, followed by over 300 in the ensuing years.

Rockwell left school in the tenth grade to study at the National Academy of Design and the Art Students League. When World War I broke out Rockwell, eager for action,

enlisted in the Navy but when his association with the *Post* was discovered he was assigned to sketching Naval officers and visitors. Returning to civilian life, he grew in popularity as his clients multiplied. His illustrations, full of warmth and homespun humor, appeared in magazines, ads, posters, calendars and books. He also received commissions to paint portraits of several U.S. Presidents and prominent world figures.

While Rockwell's painting style was always impeccable, it was his ability to get the viewer emotionally involved in his pictures that instilled him in the hearts of Americans. During World War II Rockwell's "Four Freedoms" posters were instrumental in raising $132 million through the sale of War Bonds. One of the series, "Freedom of Speech," is in the collection of the Metropolitan Museum of Art. His "Freedom from Fear,"

shown at right, demonstrates how he achieved a feeling of peace through the loving, relaxed poses of the models, a subdued palette, and soft lighting. The warm shaft of light in the stairwell draws attention to the fact that it's evening and the scene takes place in an upstairs bedroom.

In 1958 Rockwell became the first illustrator to be inducted into the Society of Illustrators Hall of Fame, and the following year he was named "Artist of the Year" by the Artists Guild of New York.

Rockwell moved to Stockbridge, Massachusetts, in 1959, and eventually to Vermont. The Norman Rockwell Museum at Stockbridge is a tribute to this beloved American whose art touched the lives of millions.

"Willie Takes a Step," inside illustration for American *magazine, January 1935. Collection of The Norman Rockwell Museum at Stockbridge.*

"Triple Self Portrait," cover illustration for The Saturday Evening Post, *February 13, 1960. © 1960 by The Curtis Publishing Company. Collection of The Norman Rockwell Museum at Stockbridge.*

"Breaking Home Ties," cover illustration for The Saturday Evening Post, *September 25, 1954. © 1954 by The Curtis Publishing Company. Collection of The Norman Rockwell Museum at Stockbridge.*

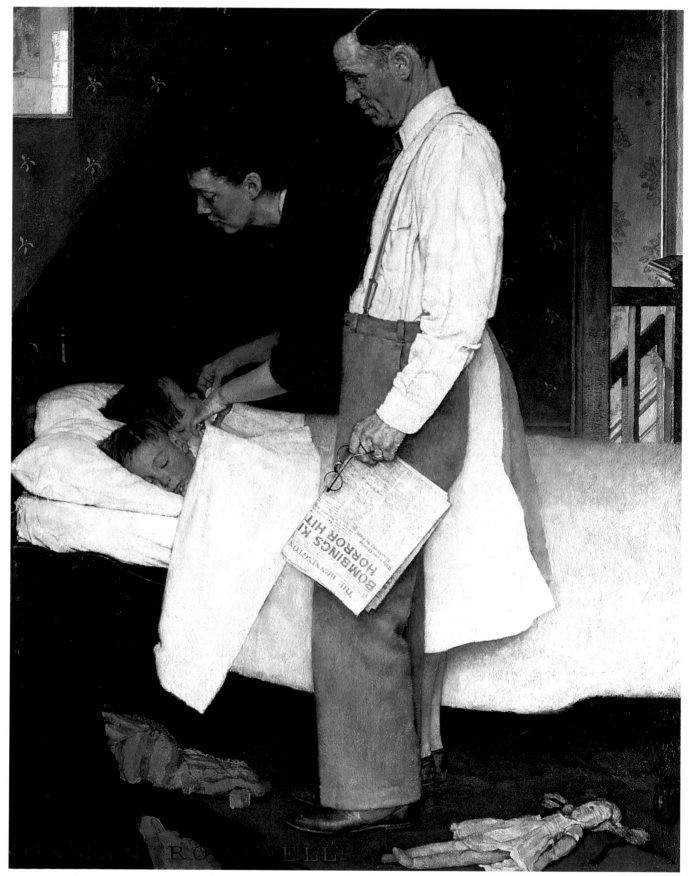

"Freedom from Fear," illustration for The Saturday Evening Post, *March 13, 1943. Collection of The Norman Rockwell Museum at Stockbridge.*

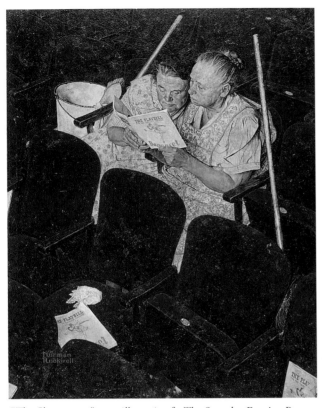

"The Charwomen," cover illustration for The Saturday Evening Post, *April 6, 1946. © 1946 by The Curtis Publishing Company. Private collection.*

"Spring/Winter," cover illustration for Boys' Life, *April 1934. © 1934 by Boys' Life. Reproduction courtesy of The Norman Rockwell Museum at Stockbridge.*

"Scout Memories," calendar illustration for the Boy Scouts of America, 1932. Photo courtesy of the Archives of the American Illustrators Gallery, New York City.

"Freedom of Speech," illustration for The Saturday Evening Post, *February 21, 1943. Collection of The Norman Rockwell Museum at Stockbridge.*

Known as the "Dean of Illustrators," Dean Cornwell earned the title through his work as teacher, lecturer, illustrator, and muralist.

Born in Kentucky, where his ancestors were among the earliest settlers, Cornwell retained a deep interest in American history, which was reflected in his work throughout his lifetime. While still in his teens he won first prize in a contest and received $1 for his first published drawing.

At age 19 Cornwell left for Chicago to work at *The Chicago American* and later the *Chicago Tribune*. In 1915 he moved to New York to study at the Art Students League. There he met Harvey Dunn, who became his mentor and instilled in him the philosophy of Howard Pyle with whom Dunn had studied.

From 1916 through the 1930s Cornwell's illustrations appeared in a multitude of popular magazines. In the mid-1920s he toured the Middle East, photographing and sketching, and used the material as reference for his illustrations for "The Man of Galilee," one of which is shown opposite, and "The City of the Great King." Cornwell claimed that the overwhelming sunlight of that area was like no other and that even oil paint taken straight from the tube could not match the brilliance of the color seen there.

Hearst Publications offered him a contract for $100,000 which Cornwell turned down. He reasoned that in order to attain immortality as an artist, he must concentrate on painting murals. He entered and won a competition to paint a series of murals for the Los Angeles Public Library. With no space large enough for the project, Cornwell contacted Frank Brangwyn in England, with whom he had previously apprenticed, who invited him to use his studio in London. The mural, consisting of over 300 figures, took five years to complete and cost Cornwell far more than the $50,000 he received. Cornwell went on to paint dozens of murals for government buildings, hotels, corporations, and airlines.

Cornwell served as president of the Society of Illustrators from 1922 to 1926 and was elected to the Illustrators Hall of Fame in 1959.

"Gallows Key," illustration for Cosmopolitan *magazine, August 1930. Photo courtesy of Illustration House, Inc.*

"World War I Doughboy." Collection of the Society of Illustrators Museum of American Illustration.

"The Enchanted Hill," illustration for Cosmopolitan *magazine, November 1924. Collection of Alan Goffman.*

"The Man of Galilee." Photo courtesy of Illustration House, Inc.

"Tiger Tiger," illustration for Cosmopolitan *magazine, 1938. Collection of the Society of Illustrators Museum of American Illustration.*

"The Robe." The Charles Martignette Collection.

Detail drawing of the commissioner in the "Treaty of Lancaster" mural at right. Collection of Mr. and Mrs. Gerald McConnell.

"The Treaty of Lancaster" mural. The collection of the Detroit Athletic Club.

Preliminary sketch.
Private collection.

Illustration for General Motors
World War II advertisement. The
Charles Martignette Collection.

Orphaned at the age of 5, Harold Von Schmidt was brought up in California by his grandfather, a Forty-niner, whose stories of the old West fascinated the boy. As a young man, Von Schmidt worked as a lumberjack and cowhand. These early influences were reflected in his paintings throughout his lifetime.

Von Schmidt's pursuit of an art career began with studies at the San Francisco Art Institute and the California College of Arts. He went on to become art director at Foster & Kleiser, and il-lustrated for *Sunset* magazine. During World War I he made posters for the U.S. Navy, and during World War II he became an artist-correspondent for the U.S. Air Force and for King Features Syndicate.

In 1924 Von Schmidt moved East to further study with Harvey Dunn, who taught him to paint the epic rather than the incident. In the years that followed, his illustrations, full of action and drama, appeared in virtually all the magazines. On the facing page a tense moment is depicted by isolating the boy in the center of the painting and surrounding him with alli-gators, giving the boy hero status.

Twelve of Von Schmidt's paintings of the Gold Rush hang in the Sacramento, California, Governor's office and five of his Civil War paintings are in the collection of West Point Military Academy. He was an officer of the American Indian Defense Association, and in 1968 was awarded the first Gold Medal by the National Cowboy Hall of Fame. As an avid athlete, Von Schmidt was a member of the American Olympic Rugby Football Team in 1920.

During his many years as a resident of Westport, Connecticut, he was very active in civic affairs and was a founding faculty member of the Famous Artists Schools based there. He served as President of the Society of Illustrators from 1938 to 1941.

*"GIs in Korea."
Collection of the
Society of Illustrators
Museum of American
Illustration.*

*"The Pali on Oahu."
Collection of the Society
of Illustrators Museum of
American Illustration.*

"The Dark River," illustration for The Saturday Evening Post, *May 28, 1936. The Charles Martignette Collection.*

"The Hunter Hunted." Photo courtesy of Illustration House, Inc.

"Introducing the New Foreman." Private Collection.

"Nathan Hale." Collection of Mr. and Mrs. Gerald McConnell.

"Horse Race," illustration for Esquire *magazine, 1950. Collection of the Society of Illustrators Museum of American Illustration.*

"Homage to Frederic Remington," illustration for John Hancock Mutual Life Insurance Company advertisement.

(1 8 8 1 - 1 9 6 2)

Self taught, Fred G. Cooper was a calligrapher, humorist, designer, teacher, philosopher, and considered a pixie by his friends. The editor of the old *Life* magazine, where Cooper once served as art director, claimed that Cooper had two brains in one: the right frontal brain lobe, mathematical, exact, and scientific; the left lobe completely cuckoo.

Born in Oregon, Cooper inherited the vitality of his pioneer parents and in his eighty years made a substantial contribution to the arts. From Oregon he moved to San Francisco and five years later, in 1904, to New York where he attained his first success as a theatre poster artist. When World War I broke out he produced posters for the war effort, then went on to turn out cartoons and verse that made his stylized lower-case initials f.g.c. familiar to all. He worked with Oswald Cooper (no relation) in producing the Cooper Bold and Cooper Black type faces.

Cooper was influenced by the graphics of Lautrec, William Nicholson and Edward Penfield. Like Lautrec, he could distill a subject down to its simplest form, eliminating anything that was not absolutely essential. The poster of the couple on the opposite page could not be more direct—with a few bold, black and white shapes he said it all.

He created a trademark for Con Edison, a quaint little Colonial character, which keyed most of their advertising, posters and promotional work, and which he revised dozens of times over the years. He did covers for *Life* and *Collier's*, along with countless humorous little black-and-white topical decorations for *Life* editorials.

Cooper's art, like his wit, was spontaneous—so much a part of him that it defied being analyzed, explained or copied.

Personal Christmas greeting poster, 1925.

"The Edison family Dines Out," 1908.

Early illustration for N.Y. Edison Company, 1907.

Cooper drew this elegant illustration for the Edison Weekly, *1906.*

Poster for New York Edison Company, 1928.

Cover for unpublished book by F.G. Cooper, late 1930s. Poster for New York Edison Company, 1928.

Illustration for the Edison Weekly, *1906.*

Poster for The Electrical Exposition and Motor Show of 1914.

All art courtesy of Leslie Cabarga, author of The Lettering and Graphic Design of F.G. Cooper, *published by Art Direction Book Company.*

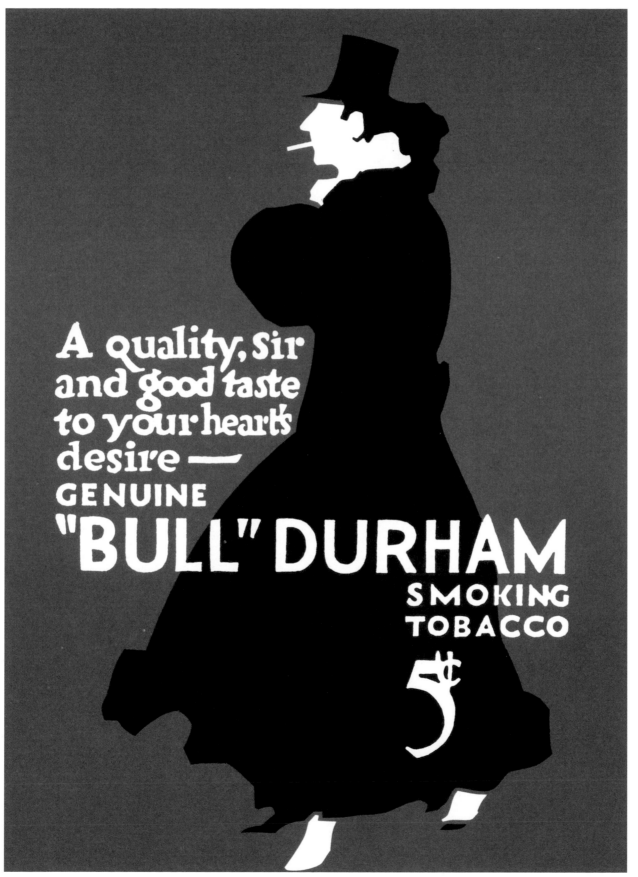

Poster for American Tobacco Co., c. 1928.

F L O Y D   D A V I S

The exaggerated gesture of the central figure in the picture on the facing page, and the animated reactions of the audience, reflect Floyd MacMillan Davis's knack for depicting his characters with warm humor. He felt caricature and some distortion were more arresting and much more fun in illustration than literal interpretations, and relied almost wholly on his retentive memory and remarkable imagination for his material.

A modest man, Davis attributed much of his success to the critical judgement of his wife, Gladys Rockmore Davis, a respected painter in her own right. Davis never had the benefit of a formal art education. Forced by circumstance to quit high school at the end of his first year, he got a job as an apprentice in a Chicago lithography shop for $3 a week and was given an opportunity to develop his own drawing skills. From there he went to work for Meyer Both & Co., a Chicago art service.

His career was interrupted by two-and-a-half years of service in the U.S. Navy during World War I. When he returned to Chicago he joined the Grauman Brothers studio where he met Gladys Rockmore, a successful fashion artist who also worked there. He became so infatuated with her and so distracted that his output of work dwindled to the point where the management finally asked the young lady to leave. She and Davis were married in 1925 and a year later moved to New York, where Davis was kept busy doing advertising illustrations depicting haughty society types.

In the 1930s, however, Davis's work for the magazines dealt with humbler subjects—pictures of southern rural and hill people for stories by such authors as William Faulkner and MacKinlay Kantor.

With the outbreak of World War II, Davis served as an artist-correspondent for the War Department. Many of those paintings were reproduced by *Life* magazine as part of a pictorial record of the war and now hang in the Pentagon in Washington, D.C.

"Graduation Day: An Old American Tradition," full-page advertisement for H.J. Heinz, published in The Saturday Evening Post, *1945. The Charles Martignette Collection.*

"The Ultimatum," illustration for King of the Mountains, *January 7, 1939. Collection of the Society of Illustrators Museum of American Illustration.*

"Last Act, Last Scene," illustration for The Saturday Evening Post, *1929. Sanford Low Memorial Collection of American Illustration, New Britain Museum of American Art.*

Edward Arthur Wilson's lifelong fascination with the sea took root when he was a child. His family was in the shipping business and had moved from Glasgow, Scotland, where he was born, to Rotterdam, Holland. Every day he watched ships sailing to and from the four corners of the world and was captivated by the romance of the sea. When he was seven years old, the family moved to America and settled in Chicago, Illinois.

Wilson studied at the Chicago Art Institute and in 1909 went on to study for two years with Howard Pyle in Wilmington, Delaware. Instead of returning to Chicago, he moved to New York and began his career as an advertising illustrator, working on campaigns for clients such as LaSalle, Cadillac and Victrola. During this period he also illustrated for most of the major magazines.

The three automobile advertisements on these pages are fine examples of Wilson's clean, uncluttered style. His beautifully rendered cars, as well as buildings, landscape and people, are all drawn in neat, precise lines and painted in simple color washes. A wonderful sense of crispness and purity pervades his illustrations—small wonder that advertisers loved his work.

In 1921, a publisher saw a woodcut of a sailor Wilson had made as a Christmas card and commissioned him to illustrate *Iron Men and Wooden Ships*, a collection of sea chanteys—songs that sailors sing while working. Wilson's work drew critical praise and when, in 1930, The Limited Editions Club published his illustrations for *Robinson Crusoe*, his fame as a book illustrator was established. Over the next several years he illustrated well over sixty books, among which were: *Fall and By*, a collection of drinking songs; *The Pirate's Treasure*, which he also wrote; *The Rime of the Ancient Mariner*; *Two Years Before the Mast*; *The Tempest*; *Green Mansions*; *Anthony Adverse* and *Treasure Island*.

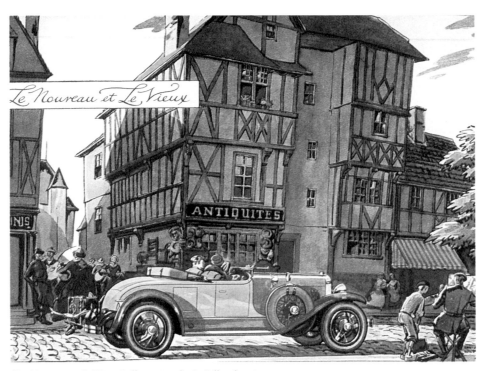

"Le Nouveau et Le Vieux," illustration for LaSalle advertisement.

"Windemere," illustration for boat advertisement.

Illustration for Dewar's "White Label" Scotch Whiskies.

"Mont St. Michel," illustration for Cadillac-LaSalle advertisement.

"A Finer and Far More Distinguished LaSalle," illustration for LaSalle V-8.

A Southern gentleman in the truest sense of the word, Walter Biggs's paintings reflected his genteel upbringing and his artistic sensitivity. His interest in art became apparent when, before he was even a teenager, he took a correspondence course in pen-and-ink drawing. At the age of 17 Biggs left Virginia, where he grew up, and headed for New York. There he enrolled at the Chase School and studied under Robert Henri, Edward Penfield and Lucius Hitchcock. His classmates, Edward Hopper, George Bellows, Guy Pene Dubois, Rockwell Kent, and Eugene Speicher, all went on to become famous as well.

Within a year of arriving in New York, one of Biggs's illustrations appeared in *Young's Magazine*, followed by another in *Field and Stream*. By 1906 he was much sought after, and over the ensuing years he illustrated for most of the magazines then in vogue.

Working out of a cluttered studio in a building where Lincoln Center now stands, Biggs created richly colored, beautiful scenes inspired by his homeland—the Southern churches, homes, people and places whose images he carried in his mind and heart. The vivid impressionistic painting on the opposite page is a splendid example of the emotional feelings Biggs was able to instill in his work. His loose painting style added excitement to whatever action was taking place in the illustration. As his paintings became more impressionistic, he began exhibiting in art galleries as well. His work was shown regularly at the National Academy, the Salmagundi Club, the American Watercolor Society and the Philadelphia Watercolor Society.

Biggs also taught at the Art Students League and the Grand Central School of Art. By the time he was inducted into the Society of Illustrators Hall of Fame in 1963, Biggs had moved back to Virginia where he continued to paint for his own pleasure.

Photo courtesy of Illustration House, Inc.

"The Preacher." Collection of the Society of Illustrators Museum of American Illustration.

"Alonzo Williams in his Studio." Collection of the Society of Illustrators Museum of American Illustration.

"Gospel Meeting," illustration for Cosmopolitan *magazine, c. 1932. Photo courtesy of Illustration House, Inc.*

During more than five decades of illustrating, Arthur William Brown, or "Brownie" as he was known, kept current with the changing styles of each period, portraying the smart set with the pizzaz so vital to magazine art of that era. The five illustrations shown on these pages span thirty years of America's changing fashions and illustration styles. The artist at her easel was drawn in 1915, the couple in evening attire in 1922, the threesome in front of a dressing table in 1936, the beach scene in 1940, and the woman in red in 1941. Brownie traded pencil for pen in the 1940s and began adding more color to his drawings.

Born in Hamilton, Ontario, Brown quit school at age 14 and took a job on a Canadian steamer where he spent a good deal of time sketching. On his return to Hamilton he sold the drawings to a local newspaper and began freelancing. Although he was earning only $3.50 a week, he was able to save enough so that in 1901 he left for New York in a cut-down suit of his uncle's and $400 in his pocket.

Brown enrolled at the Art Students League and studied under Walter Appleton Clark. Hearing that a friend had been commissioned by *The Saturday Evening Post* to write an article about the circus, Brown decided to tag along and spent six weeks sketching the circus. The *Post* liked the drawings and bought them. Thus began Brown's association with that publication, which lasted for over forty years.

Through the next decades he illustrated stories by Clarence Budington Kelland, Irvin S. Cobb, Ring Lardner, Rose Franken, and collaborated with O. Henry, Booth Tarkington and Sinclair Lewis. He drew Arthur Train's Ephraim Tutt, F. Scott Fitzgerald's flappers and the first airmen's fashions for Montague Glass's early aviation stories.

Brown joined the Society of Illustrators during Charles Dana Gibson's presidency, served as President of the Society from 1944 to 1947, was elected to the Hall of Fame in 1964, and acted as Honorary President until his death in 1966.

"House of Cards," illustration for The Saturday Evening Post, *July 1940. Collection of the Society of Illustrators Museum of American Illustration.*

"The Audition," 1941. Collection of the Society of Illustrators Museum of American Illustration.

"Artist at Easel," 1915. Collection of the Society of Illustrators Museum of American Illustration.

Collection of the Society of Illustrators Museum of American Illustration.

Collection of the Society of Illustrators Museum of American Illustration.

Throughout his lifetime, Alfred Charles Parker's two passions were art and music. He helped pay his way through the St. Louis School of Fine Arts at Washington University by playing saxophone in a jazz band on a Mississippi riverboat.

A native of St. Louis, Parker worked in an art studio after completing art school and eventually opened his own studio. An illustration for a 1931 *House Beautiful* cover was his first job to appear nationally. Elated, he sent three pencil drawings of girls' heads to *The Ladies' Home Journal* and all three were bought. There

followed assignments from leading magazines such as *McCall's*, *Collier's* and *Cosmopolitan*.

In the mid-thirties Parker moved to New York where his innovative illustrations enchanted publishers and public alike. He managed to stay one step ahead of his imitators—his work always changing, always startling. He was so versatile that he once illustrated a whole issue of *Cosmopolitan* using a different name and style for each story.

A mother-daughter cover which Parker painted for *The Ladies' Home Journal* in 1939 was the first of a series which became so famous that it set a new style for mother-daughter fashions. Parker was a trend-setter, and every item in his illustrations—whether props, decor or dress—reflected his excellent taste. He became a natural choice for the American

Airlines ad campaign in which he portrayed fashionable, happy travelers. The mother and baby shown opposite, for instance, couldn't better express the message the airline hoped to convey—that flying in their planes was a joyful, carefree experience. Parker used a fairly simple palette and kept his brushwork to a minimum, allowing his incredible sense of design to take over.

A resident of Westport, Connecticut, for many years, Parker was a founding member of the Famous Artists Schools located there. Eventually he moved his family to Carmel, California, where he continued to work occasionally for *Boys' Life* and *Sports Illustrated*. Winner of countless awards, Parker was elected to the Society's Hall of Fame in 1965.

IllIllustration for McCall's *magazine. Collection of the Society of Illustrators Museum of American Illustration.*

"Palm Court—Plaza Hotel," advertisement for American Airlines DC7, c. 1950s. Collection of the Society of Illustrators Museum of American Illustration.

"Carnig," illustration for Good Housekeeping *magazine, 1952. Collection of Arpi Ermoyan.*

Illustration for The Ladies' Home Journal. *Collection of the Society of Illustrators Museum of American Illustration.*

Illustration for The Ladies' Home Journal. *Collection of the Society of Illustrators Museum of American Illustration.*

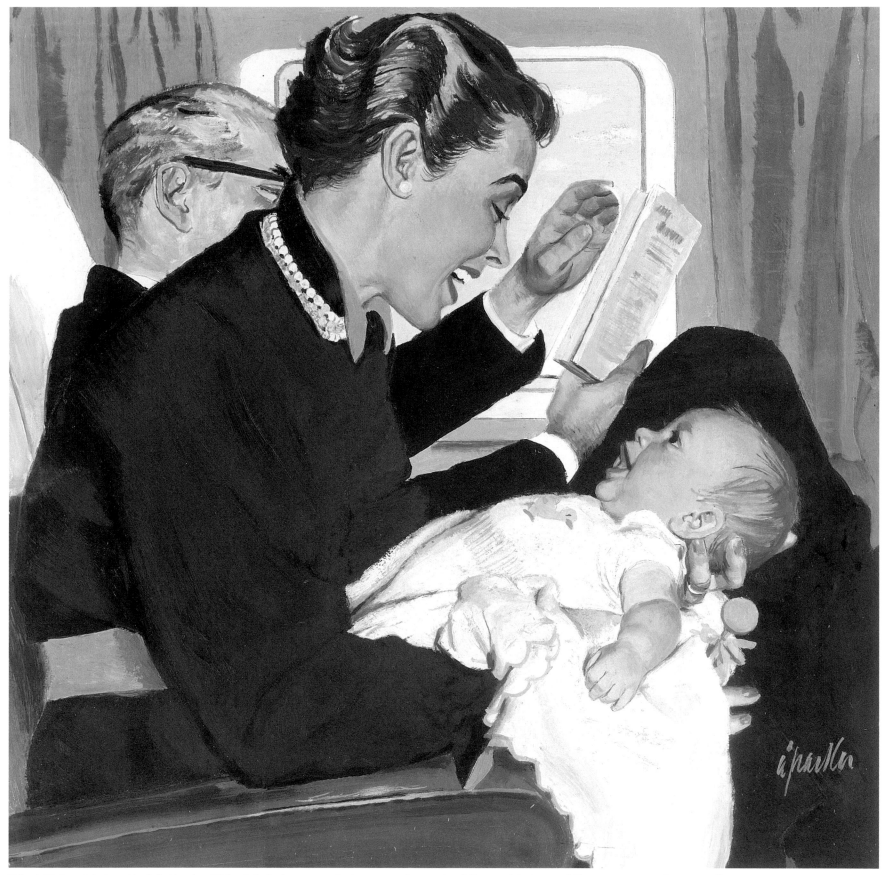

"There's Nothing Like It on Earth for Traveling With a Baby," advertisement for American Airlines, 1949. Collection of the Society of Illustrators Museum of American Illustration.

Complicated illustrations filled with highly animated characters in exaggerated poses could be easily recognized as the work of Albert Dorne. He worked rather small because he believed that in small scale one was less likely to put in unnecessary details, and that the probability of faithful reproduction would be greater. His medium of choice was colored inks, which he applied with great skill after making meticulous pencil drawings in line.

Dorne's life was a true "rags to riches" story. As a poor but enterprising "Dead End Kid," he grew up on New York City's Lower East Side and left school in the seventh grade to help support his family. He worked as a newsboy, an office boy, a prize fighter, an art studio assistant, then rose to become a highly respected illustrator, teacher and entrepreneur. Although he had no training in art, he nevertheless became one of the country's most successful advertising illustrators, earning top dollar while still in his twenties. Small wonder then, that in 1963 the American Schools and Colleges Association awarded him the Horatio Alger Award For Achievement.

Aside from his thriving illustration career, Dorne's accomplishments were many. He was co-founder of the Code of Ethics and Fair Practices, and in 1947 served a term as president of the Society of Illustrators. In 1948, eager to help aspiring artists, he called together 12 of the most prominent and successful illustrators and formed the Famous Artists Schools in Westport, Connecticut. Most of the founding members are now in the Illustrators Hall of Fame. With their vast knowledge and experience, the lessons and critiques offered by those instructors produced another generation of professional illustrators. Dorne, as founder-director, was the driving force behind that home study course.

In 1953 Dorne was awarded the first Gold Medal for "a distinguished career" from the New York Art Directors Club, in 1958 he received an honorary Doctor of Fine Arts degree from Adelphi College, and the Society of Illustrators elected him to its Hall of Fame in 1966.

"Mr. Botts—Tractor Salesman." Collection of the Society of Illustrators Museum of American Illustration.

Illustration for The Saturday Evening Post. *Collection of the Society of Illustrators Museum of American Illustration.*

Illustration for Wurlitzer advertisement, 1946. The Charles Martignette Collection.

Because of his masterful drafts-manship and superb compositions, Robert Fawcett was considered "the illustrator's illustrator" by his colleagues. His attention to detail, whether portraying a character, a room setting or a costume, was thorough and precise. His passion for detail is apparent in the illustration on the facing page. Whether drawn in pencil, pen or brush, he possessed total control of line, while color played a secondary role in his illustrations. The fact that he was colorblind in no way diminished his ability to use color values effectively and may, in fact, have contributed to the development of his particular style.

Born in London, Fawcett was encouraged by his father, an amateur artist, to begin drawing at an early age. When the family moved to Canada, Fawcett, then 14, quit school and took a job in an engraving shop. A few years later they moved to New York where Fawcett, having accumulated a thousand dollars, sailed for London and enrolled at the Slade School. For two years he drew incessantly under rigorous discipline, soaked up the culture offered by London's museums, theaters and concerts, and made trips to France where he absorbed the work of the modernists.

Returning to New York in 1924, he began illustrating for magazines and advertising agencies, which kept him busy for the next few decades. His drawings for the Sherlock Holmes series in *Collier's* magazine in the 1950s were remarkable. The backgrounds of late Victorian England, the intricately-drawn interiors and period costumes showed Fawcett's extraordinary ability to create striking settings and evoke dramatic moods.

For *Look* magazine Fawcett created an outstanding group of illustrations for MacKinlay Kantor's article, "If the South had Won the Civil War," and for the Commonwealth Institute of London he painted a series of murals.

A founding faculty member of the Famous Artists Schools in Westport, Connecticut, Fawcett was also a member of the Society of Illustrators and was inducted into the Illustrators Hall of Fame in 1967, the first to be so honored posthumously.

"The Personal Experiences of a Young Doctor," illustration for Collier's *magazine, 1951. Collection of the Society of Illustrators Museum of American Illustration.*

"The Adventure of the Abbas Ruby," illustration for Collier's *magazine, 1953. Photo courtesy of Illustration House, Inc.*

"Nude." Collection of the Society of Illustrators Museum of American Illustration.

"Cool Customer," illustration for Collier's *magazine, 1951. Collection of the Society of Illustrators Museum of American Illustration.*

"Design for Terror," illustration for Collier's *magazine, April 1, 1955. Collection of Mr. and Mrs. Gerald McConnell.*

Known as the Dean of American automotive art, Peter Helck's passion for automobiles began when, as a teenager, he watched early racing competitions. He was especially thrilled by the Vanderbilt Cup Race of 1908. Little did he realize then, that he would someday be the proud owner of the very vehicle which had won that race—the 1906 Locomobile Racing Car, "Old No. 16"—one of the most famous automobiles in history.

Born and raised in New York City, Helck attended the Art Students League. In 1920 he went abroad to study with Frank Brangwyn in England, did some British motor advertising while there, then went on to Spain, dividing his time between study, painting and illustrating for Madrid agencies. After many sketching trips through Europe and Africa, he returned to England where he opened a studio and worked for British and American clients. By 1927 he was back in New York, illustrating for industrial firms.

Thanks to his thorough mechanical knowledge, his illustrations of locomotives, automobiles, trucks and farm equipment were painted with great authenticity. His preliminary sketches were completely worked out, right down to the last bolt and rivet. His brush worked well for him in keeping the mechanical objects in his pictures from seeming slick. Dirty and dented, his racing cars appear to have been on the speedway many times before, and his ability to show a car moving at great speed is evident in the picture on the facing page.

Helck did a series of eight spreads depicting early auto racing for *Esquire*, one of many magazines for whom he worked. He was author-illustrator of two books on racing: *The Checkered Flag*, published in 1961, and *Great Auto Races*, published in 1975. In a large barn on his farm in Boston Corners, New York, Helck housed an historical collection of antique cars. He was also a founding faculty member of the Famous Artists Schools in Westport, Connecticut.

"1908 Vanderbilt Cup Race." Photo courtesy of Illustration House, Inc.

"Gandy Dancer." Photo courtesy of Illustration House, Inc.

"The Regenmeister," 1938. Collection of the Society of Illustrators Museum of American Illustration.

With his fresh, innovative style Austin Briggs introduced a spontaneous element to illustration. His subjects are caught in candid poses—they are real people, moving in a real world. The couple on the facing page has been captured in an exuberant moment as they depart from a plane. Briggs worked in a wide range of techniques and media, and managed to keep one step ahead of his many imitators by constantly experimenting and reinventing his approach to illustration.

The first gallery to exhibit his work was the private railroad car in which he was born in Humboldt, Minnesota. He began drawing at the age of four and filled the car with his artwork. His father installed telegraphic systems in railroad cars, and moved the family along from job to job. This modest beginning was a far cry from the home in Connecticut which noted architect Elliot Noyes designed for Briggs many years later.

When Briggs was 12 the family moved to Detroit, where he won a scholarship to the Wicker Art School. At 17 he apprenticed with an art service and made some drawings for the *Dearborn Independent*. With those samples in hand, Briggs moved East and got assignments from *Collier's*, *McClure's* and *Pictorial Review*, and enrolled in the Art Students League to study under George Bridgman.

During the next few years Briggs did movie posters, worked for the pulps, ghosted drawings for the "Flash Gordon" comic strip, and illustrated for *Blue Book* and *Amazing Stories* magazines. His work finally caught the attention of art directors of magazines such as *Redbook*, *Cosmopolitan* and *The Saturday Evening Post*, as well as major advertising agencies. From that point on, Briggs became a dominant force in illustration.

While traveling in Europe in the 1960s, Briggs became enamored with the beauty and lifestyle of Paris, where he eventually moved and where he spent the last years of his life.

Briggs was a founding faculty member of the Famous Artists Schools in Westport, Connecticut, and won numerous awards in the Society of Illustrators' annual exhibitions.

"The City," illustration for Lithopinion *magazine. Photo courtesy of Illustration House, Inc.*

"Boating in the Rapids," illustration for Sports Illustrated. *Collection of the Society of Illustrators Museum of American Illustration.*

"General Omar Bradley in Vietnam." *Collection of the Society of Illustrators Museum of American Illustration.*

Illustration for American Airlines advertisement. Photo courtesy of Illustration House, Inc.

(1 8 8 3 - 1 9 7 0)

So worldwide is Rube Goldberg's reputation that an entry in Webster's Dictionary after his name reads: "designating any very complicated invention, machine, scheme, etc. laboriously contrived to perform a seemingly simple operation." Such an example is his "Perpetual Motion Machine," opposite. Making light of serious subjects, such as taxes, in a wildly humorous manner endeared him to the public and momentarily took the curse off dreaded or controversial topics. It was great fun to follow the thought process of his zany inventions which were drawn so cleverly and with such directness that a punch line was hardly necessary.

Goldberg was also a serious editorial cartoonist, artist, writer of songs, books and plays, and invented phrases such as "No matter how thin you slice it, it's still baloney," which became part of our language.

Reuben Lucius Goldberg was born in San Francisco and graduated from the University of California, where he had studied to become a mining engineer. After a year of drawing sewer pipes for a living, he gave up engineering in 1904 and became a sports cartoonist for the *San Francisco Chronicle*, the *San Francisco Bulletin* and, in 1907, the *New York Mail*. By 1916 he was earning more than $100,000 a year as a creator of syndicated comic strips such as "Boob McNutt," "Lala Palooza"

and "Mike and Ike—They Look Alike."

In 1938, Goldberg became an editorial cartoonist for the *New York Sun*, and ten years later won the Pulitzer Prize for a cartoon warning of the perils of atomic weapons. When the *Sun* folded in 1950, he joined the *Journal-American* and stayed with the Hearst newspaper until its demise. He then worked for King Features Syndicate until his retirement from cartooning in 1964.

At the age of 80, Goldberg began a new career as a sculptor, calling his little statues "kindly" rather than satirical. He was also one of the founders of the National Cartoonists Society and for years a very active member of the Society of Illustrators.

"Peace Today," illustration for the New York Sun, *1947. Winner of the Pulitzer Prize, 1948. Reproduced in* Rube Goldberg vs The Machine Age, *published by Hastings House, 1968.*

"Whiskers," published by Jerome Remick & Co. Collection of the Society of Illustrators Museum of American Illustration.

"Be Your Own Dentist." Reproduced in Rube Goldberg vs. The Machine Age, *published by Hastings House.*

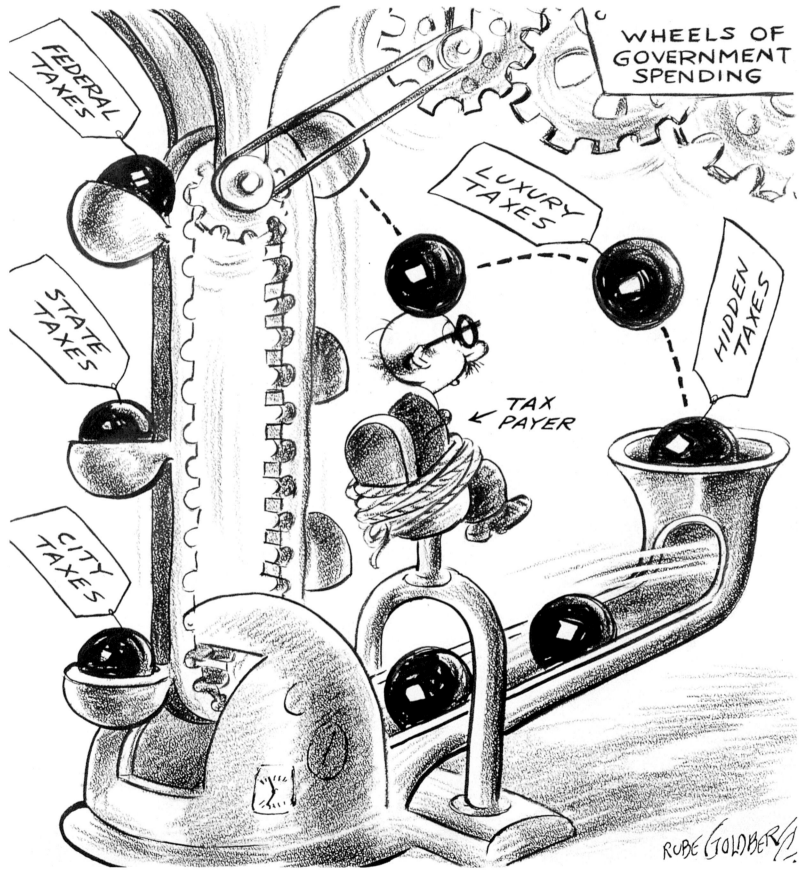

"Perpetual Motion." Photo courtesy of the Society of Illustrators Archives.

As a realist painter of Americana, Stevan Dohanos was best known for the human interest pictures he created during World War II and on through the Cold War years. *The Saturday Evening Post* became an ideal showcase for him, his first cover appearing in 1943, followed by 124 covers during the 1940s and 1950s. Americans identified with his paintings of ordinary people in everyday situations which often reflected Dohanos's wry sense of humor. For the most part his models were local citizens and backgrounds were scenes of the town in which he lived. In the

Post cover on the opposite page he elicits our sympathy for the apartment dweller who has been rudely awakened by early morning painters.

A native of Ohio, at 19 Dohanos enrolled in night classes at the Cleveland School of Art and worked in art studios by day. Winning prizes in national exhibitions brought him recognition and a commission in 1936 from the Treasury Department to paint murals for various federal buildings. With this success, and a one-man show in New York, Dohanos moved East in 1938, settling in Westport, Connecticut.

He was commissioned to design the 1941 Christmas Seal for the National Tuberculosis Association, and in 1959 the U.S. Postal Service asked him to design a stamp commemorating

the 10th anniversary of NATO. As Design Coordinator of the Citizen's Stamp Advisory Committee from 1961 to 1981, he created 40 stamps himself and commissioned over 300 by other artists. For his many years of service, the Postal Service dedicated the Hall of Stamps in Washington, D.C. in his honor.

Retiring from commercial work in 1983, he traveled and painted for sheer pleasure. His work is in many museum and private collections, and a retrospective of his work, "Images of America," was held at the New Britain Museum of American Art in 1985.

Dohanos was a founding faculty member of the Famous Artists Schools in Westport. He served as President of the Society of Illustrators from 1961 to 1963, and as Honorary President from 1982 until his death in 1994.

Poster for the American Red Cross. Collection of the American Red Cross.

"The Coal Men," cover illustration for The Saturday Evening Post. *Collection of the Society of Illustrators Museum of American Illustration.*

"Chains of Fear," cover illustration for The Saturday Evening Post, *1958. Collection of the Society of Illustrators Museum of American Illustration.*

"Early Morning Painters," cover illustration for The Saturday Evening Post. *Collection of the Society of Illustrators Museum of American Illustration.*

Born in Mulo on the Bay of Catarro in Yugoslavia, Ray Prohaska's early exposure to the life of fishermen forever instilled in him a love of the sea. For many years, and until his death, Prohaska lived in Amagansett, Long Island, where he painted and fished, and where the local fishermen considered him not only a highly respected artist, but one of their very own. The two scenes of fishermen on these pages show his versatility and how his style ranged from very painterly to the abstract.

When he was eight, his father, an officer in the Austrian army, moved the family to America and settled in San Francisco where, at the age of 18, Prohaska entered the California School of Fine Arts. Following his studies there he began getting commercial work from Grauman Studios and advertising agencies such as J. Walter Thompson and N.W. Ayer.

In 1929 Prohaska moved to New York where he received his first editorial assignments from *The Delineator* and *Woman's Home Companion*. Manuscripts from most all major magazines soon followed. He also produced many paintings and drawings for Shell Oil, Maxwell House Coffee, John Hancock Life Insurance, and scores of other advertising accounts.

Prohaska taught at the Art Students League in 1961 and urged his students to draw from life—not only in the studio, but on the street, in the subway, in the home—until it became, like handwriting, a record of feelings and events. He believed in exhaustive experimentation in various mediums and kept current on the latest fashions in clothing and décor.

In addition to his illustrations, Prohaska painted for exhibition as well and won several prizes, including the Hallmark Award in 1949, the Audubon Medal in 1954, Grumbacher First Prize in 1958 and a Gold Medal from the Society of Illustrators in 1963. From 1964 to 1969 he was Artist-in-Residence at Washington and Lee University, where he painted a large mural depicting the communications media. Prohaska served as President of the Society of Illustrators from 1959 to 1961.

"On My Honor," illustration for The Saturday Evening Post, *1954. Collection of the Society of Illustrators Museum of American Illustration.*

"Returning Fishermen." Collection of the Society of Illustrators Museum of American Illustration.

Illustration for McCall's *magazine. Collection of the Society of Illustrators Museum of American Illustration.*

"To Walk the City Streets," illustration for The Saturday Evening Post, *April 12, 1954. Collection of the Society of Illustrators Museum of American Illustration.*

"Fisherman," 1958. Photo courtesy of the Society of Illustrators Archives.

J on Whitcomb's name conjures up images of gorgeous, starry-eyed young women. For years his sparkling illustrations lit up the pages of magazines across the nation. The large illustration shown opposite is a fine example of his style, flair for color, straightforward handling of light and shade, and his ability to compose simply and directly. A master at depicting the ideal glamorous American woman, he enhanced his illustrations with the latest fashions in dress and decor. While he attracted many imitators, he remained a leader of this particular genre of illustration.

Born in Oklahoma and raised in Wisconsin, Whitcomb was fortunate in having a mother who had been an art teacher and a father who was a drafting instructor. With plenty of paints, brushes and drawing paper available, young Whitcomb began doodling and decorating his schoolbooks at an early age. He attended Ohio Wesleyan University and graduated from Ohio State where he drew pictures for the school publications and painted posters during the summer for a theater in Cleveland. After graduation he worked in a series of studios doing travel and theater posters, as well as general advertising. In 1934 he moved to New York, illustrating first for *Collier's*, then *Good Housekeeping* and many of the other popular magazines.

When World War II broke out Whitcomb joined the Navy, was commissioned a Lieutenant j.g., spent six weeks on mine sweeper duty and was eventually sent to the Pacific as a combat artist. When he returned to civilian life in 1945, *Cosmopolitan* magazine commissioned him to do a monthly series of sketches and articles about motion picture stars called "On Location with Jon Whitcomb." Working 10 to 18 hours a day, his drive and stamina allowed him to write and illustrate the column, paint a magazine cover and illustrate three stories every month.

Whitcomb lived and worked in a stunning contemporary home with a 20' x 40' studio in Darien, Connecticut. He was one of the 12 founding faculty members of the Famous Artists Schools in Westport, Connecticut.

"Playful," reproduced by Special Permission of Playboy *magazine, 1980. Copyright © 1980 by Playboy. Collection of the Society of Illustrators Museum of American Illustration.*

Magazine cover illustration, 1960. The Charles Martignette Collection.

"All About Girls," book chapter illustration for Prentis-Hall, 1962. The Charles Martignette Collection.

"Christmas," illustration for Cosmopolitan *magazine, 1957. Private collection.*

"Your Ideal Girl," *illustration for* Good Housekeeping *magazine. Photo courtesy of Illustration House, Inc.*

Praised by collector and critic alike, Tom Lovell is regarded as one of the world's finest artists of the Old West and American history. His meticulous research into clothing, weapons, lifestyle and events, plus his great knowledge of human and animal anatomy, culminate in paintings of great authenticity. In the picture on the right, for example, Lovell would have done intensive research in order to accurately depict the very bridge from which Houdini jumped, the exact clothing he wore as he was about to dive, and the correct uniforms worn by the police at that time. To set the mood of the event, he painted a gray day, maximizing the drama of the event.

Born in New York City, Lovell grew up in rural northern New Jersey. His love of literature and art prompted him to enroll in the College of Fine Arts at Syracuse University. During his junior year he began illustrating for "pulp" magazines and as a senior he did a cover plus a dozen drawings each month for Good Story Publications. As a result, work was waiting for him upon graduation.

In time, assignments from the major magazines came along. By illustrating serials by Edna Ferber, Louis Bromfield, Paul Gallico and Sinclair Lewis, Lovell gained experience in depicting period as well as character and action pictures.

In 1944 Lovell enlisted in the Marines, expecting to see action, but was assigned instead to *Leatherneck Magazine* as a staff artist and worked stateside. Some of his historical paintings are in the permanent collection of the Marine Corps, others are in the National Geographic Society, The Explorer's Club, New Britain Museum, and the headquarters of the New England, Continental and John Hancock insurance companies.

Lovell moved to Santa Fe, New Mexico, and became a regular exhibitor in the shows of Western artists held in Arizona. He won the Prix de West awarded by the National Academy of Western Art and the Gold Medal in Oil from the National Cowboy Hall of Fame.

Story illustration, 1941. Collection of the Society of Illustrators Museum of American Illustration.

Illustration for Good Housekeeping *magazine, May 1956. The Charles Martignette Collection.*

"The Blue Hour," illustration for Cosmopolitan, *1951. The Charles Martignette Collection.*

"Rescue at Sea," illustration for True *magazine. Photo courtesy of Illustration House, Inc.*

"The Jump," illustration for a story on Houdini. Photo courtesy of Illustration House, Inc.

The most famous fictional personality to emerge out of the Golden Age of Illustration was the Gibson Girl. Its creator, Charles Dana Gibson, portrayed her as a spirited, self-reliant beauty, putting an end to the Victorian clinging-vine image of womanhood. She appeared weekly in the old *Life* magazine and for 20 years Gibson Girl fashions and hair styles became the rage. Her likeness adorned everything from pillows and ashtrays to calendars and wallpaper.

Although Gibson is remembered mainly for his pictures of elegant high society types, such as those shown on these pages, many of his drawings reflected the life and idiosyncrasies of all classes. With his mastery of the penpoint, which he used almost as a brush, he "painted" the life and mores of his day with a satiric but gentle point of view. He was a communicator with whom everyone, rich or poor, could identify.

Descending from a line of New Englanders, Gibson inherited their Yankee industrious characteristics. At age 12 he received a rave review from a critic who saw his paper silhouettes in an art show. In his mid-teens he attended the Art Students League, and in 1886 sold his first drawing to *Life* for $4. Within five years he was illustrating double-page spreads in the major magazines.

Gibson sailed for London in 1889, then studied briefly at the Academie Julian in Paris. Upon his return, he was inundated with work and by 1900 was being offered staggering fees. The magazines were literally fighting over him. In 1904 a compromise was reached when *Collier's Weekly* signed Gibson to a contract for $100,000 for 100 drawings and agreed to share him with *Life*. He became a celebrity and had the most prominent socialites of the day volunteering to pose for him.

As President of the Society of Illustrators during World War I, Gibson recruited top illustrators to design posters and billboards for the war effort. After a lifetime of working in line, this master of pen-and-ink retired to paint in oil for the last 15 years of his life.

"Bored Stiffs," illustration for Collier's *magazine, 1904, reprinted in* Everyday People. *Collection of the Society of Illustrators Museum of American Illustration.*

Portraits used in wallpaper designs. The Charles Martignette Collection.

Two-page centerfold for Life *magazine, 1901. Book cover for* A Widow and Her Friends, *1901. The Charles Martignette Collection.*

"The Blue Butterfly," illustration for Woman's Home Companion, *January 1913. The Charles Martignette Collection.*

As patriarch of the illustrious progeny which followed, Newell Convers Wyeth paved the way with his powerful paintings of pirates, cowboys, Indians and heroic literary characters. In the painting opposite, the actions of his brawny, rough cast of characters leaves no doubt in the viewer's mind as to their mission. As the group reaches the crest of the hill, the triangle formed in Wyeth's composition leads the eye to the bright red cap on the lead sacker and to the treasures they have just captured. Wyeth's gift for storytelling is immediately apparent.

Wyeth studied under his idol, Howard Pyle, and became his star pupil. Eager to gain first-hand knowledge of frontier life, Wyeth left Pennsylvania in 1904 and set out for Colorado. There he worked as a cowhand and joined the rugged life of the plains people. Later, he went to the Navajo Reservation in New Mexico where he worked for the Government as a mail-rider, making lengthy trips on horseback between stations and settlements.

Upon his return to the East, *Outing* magazine commissioned him to paint a series of illustrations portraying Indians. This was the beginning of a long and highly successful career in which Wyeth's work appeared in major magazines and in numerous books. For the *Charles Scribner's Classics* series he illustrated over 25 books, a few of which were *Treasure Island*, *Kidnapped*, *The Black Arrow*, *Mysterious Island* and *Last of the Mohicans*.

After painting in oils for many years, Wyeth changed to egg tempera and in 1939 began turning out still lifes, landscapes and portraits for exhibition. In his huge 38' x 70' Chadds Ford studio sitting atop a hillside, he painted enormous murals for insurance companies, banks, churches and government buildings.

Wyeth's untimely death occurred in a tragic railway crossing accident, ending a brilliant career in which his output of paintings is estimated to have totaled 3,000. He left behind a family of talented children, grandchildren and sons-in-law who themselves went on to great artistic acclaim.

"The Rakish Brigantine," illustration for Scribner's, *August 1914. Photo courtesy of Illustration House, Inc.*

"Spanish Galleon." Photo courtesy of Illustration House, Inc.

"Black Arrow," illustration for Scribner's, *1910. Collection of the Society of Illustrators Museum of American Illustration.*

"The Story of Gold," calendar illustration for The Romance of Commerce. *Photo courtesy of Illustration House, Inc.*

BERNIE FUCHS

(b . 1 9 3 2)

Rich, luminous colors and superb drawing mark the works of Bernie Fuchs. His impressionistic paintings arise from his fascination with the way sunlight illuminates and transforms objects into a multitude of soft colors, creating pools of light reminiscent of Vermeer. "Indian Winter," on the opposite page, is an excellent example of the way Fuchs uses sunlight and color to create the drama and mood of a picture. One can feel the frigid air, just as the Indians did, as the sun sets behind the butte.

Born in O'Fallon, Illinois, Fuchs graduated from Washington University School of Fine Arts in St. Louis. He began working for a Detroit studio where his paintings for automotive ads brought him nationwide recognition while he was still in his twenties. In 1958 Fuchs moved East and settled in Westport, Connecticut. Years later, a New York agency art director said to him, "I used to buy artwork from your father in Detroit," not realizing it had been Fuchs himself working there 25 years earlier.

Before his 30th birthday, Fuchs was named "Artist of the Year" by the Artists Guild of New York, and was commissioned to do a portrait of President Kennedy, whom he met and photographed in the Oval Office. Two of his portraits of JFK are in the Kennedy Library's permanent collection. In1975 Fuchs was elected to the Illustrators Hall of Fame, the youngest artist to be so honored.

His commissions have ranged from portraits of literary, political and theatrical celebrities to paintings of sports and historical themes. He has illustrated for major corporate clients and numerous magazines, including *McCall's*, *The New Yorker*, *Look*, *TV Guide*, and over 50 feature articles for *Sports Illustrated*. He has also designed U.S. postage stamps, illustrated children's books, and painted huge murals for international cruise ships. Having traveled extensively throughout Italy for many years, he painted his "personal view" of that country for a one-man show. Fuchs has also participated in group shows in England, Russia, Japan and galleries throughout the United States.

"Columbus," mural for the Royal Caribbean "Legend of the Seas" cruise ship, 1995.

"Spyglass Hill" at Pebble Beach, 1991. Private collection.

"Portrait of the Artist," illustration for McCall's *magazine, July 1964.*

"Indian Winter," 1991. Private collection.

"Johnny Dodd's Parlor Jazz," 1974. Private collection.

"Roman Courtyard," 1995. Collection of the artist.

"Still Life of Fruit," 1994. Collection of the artist.

Illustration for The Wolves, *published by Dial Books for Young Readers, 1996.*

"Football," illustration for ESPN, 1980.

Maxfield Parrish is revered for his beautiful landscapes and for the romantic images that arose from his incredibly fertile imagination. But above all, he is remembered for the luminous quality of his paintings. So breathtaking are his translucent blue skies, as in "Lull Brook Winter," below, that cobalt blue is sometimes referred to as "Parrish Blue." In the picture opposite, the strong contrast he created between brilliant, hot sunlight and deep shadows intensifies the drama of the scene.

Born into a family of Quakers who stressed hard work and sacrifice, Parrish developed and maintained those qualities throughout his lifetime. In 1888 he enrolled at Haverford College to study architecture, but discovered that the Quaker institution considered art an unworthy field of study. He then attended the Pennsylvania Academy of the Fine Arts in Philadelphia where he studied until 1894.

Parrish began his long and productive illustration career in Philadelphia, where he occupied studios until 1898. However, his love of the Connecticut Valley countryside prompted him to move to Windsor, Vermont, where he and his wife built a home, "The Oaks," and raised their four children.

Parrish's magazine and children's book illustrations, as well as his poster work of the 1890s, had established his reputation. Although advertisers also clamored for his work, he preferred making pictures for calendars and art prints. By the 1920s his prints were in such demand that The House of Art in New York began to commission his work specifically for reproduction in great volume. His calendars for one client were so popular that over a million reproductions were sold annually and became his primary art form for many years.

One of the many sumptuous murals which Parrish painted is the 30-foot painting depicting "Old King Cole" in the St. Regis Hotel in New York. His childhood fascination with fairy tale characters in the world of make-believe seemed to have inspired much of the subject matter in his work as an adult. During his last 30 years Parrish painted landscapes exclusively. His paintings constitute a body of work that will be cherished forever.

"Sunlit Valley," illustration for Brown & Bigelow calendar, 1950. Photo courtesy of the Archives of the American Illustrators Gallery, New York City.

"Lull Brook Winter," illustration for Brown & Bigelow executive print, 1947. Photo courtesy of the Archives of the American Illustrators Gallery, New York City.

"Morning," Easter cover for Life *magazine, April 6, 1922. Photo courtesy of the Archives of the American Illustrators Gallery, New York City.*

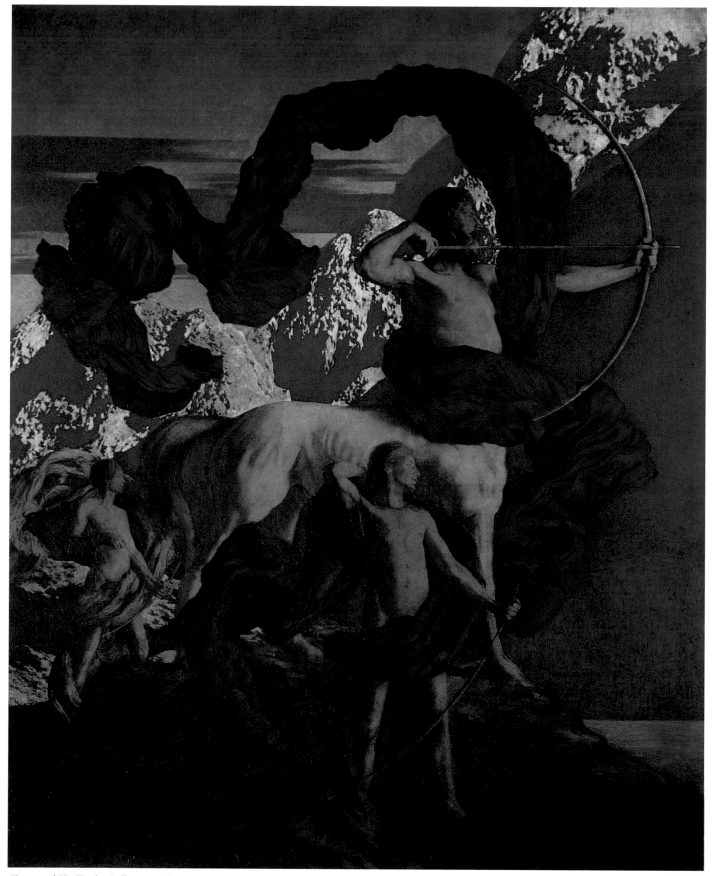

"Jason and His Teacher," illustration for A Wonder Book and Tanglewood Tales, *for* Collier's *magazine, July 23, 1910. Photo courtesy of the Archives of the American Illustrators Gallery, New York City.*

"The Glen," illustration for Brown & Bigelow calendar, 1938. Photo courtesy of the Archives of the American Illustrators Gallery, New York City.

"Jack and the Giant," cover illustration for Collier's *magazine. Collection of American Illustrators Gallery, New York City.*

"The Botanist," cover illustration for Collier's, *July 18, 1908. Collection of American Illustrators Gallery, New York City.*

"Villa Gori, Siena," illustration for Italian Villas and Their Gardens, 1904. *Collection of the Society of Illustrators Museum of American Illustration.*

"The Glen," illustration for Brown & Bigelow calendar, 1938. Photo courtesy of the Archives of the American Illustrators Gallery, New York City.

Design for the Century Mid-Summer Holiday Number, *August, 1897. Photo courtesy of the Archives of the American Illustrators Gallery, New York City.*

"Garden of Allah," decoration for gift boxes of Crane's Chocolates, 1918. Photo courtesy of the Archives of the American Illustrators Gallery, New York City.

(1 8 5 3 - 1 9 1 1)

Revered as a brilliant teacher, Howard Pyle is considered the "Father of American Illustration." He was a major force in what later came to be known as the Brandywine School. A whole generation of his students went on to become famous artists and instructors who in turn passed along his unique philosophy.

Pyle, a Quaker, was born in Wilmington, Delaware, and at age 16 enrolled in an art school in Philadelphia. He left after three years and worked in his father's business for a time while he struggled to perfect his artistic and writing skills. In 1876, an illustration he sent to *Scribner's Monthly* was accepted. Elated by this success, he set off for New York City where he quickly established himself as a professional. After three years he returned to Wilmington and, between magazine assignments, wrote and illustrated a number of books, among them *The Merry Adventures of Robin Hood*, *Book of Pirates* and *The Story of King Arthur and His Knights*. His lifelong interest in American history produced some of his greatest work; his renditions of the Revolutionary and Civil War eras remain the definitive pictures in history books.

In his painting, "The Nation Makers," Pyle skillfully expresses the great sense of spirit and fortitude of the bedraggled Revolutionary troops. His splendid composition of men marching forward to battle, undaunted, adds to the heroic aspect of the scene. A range of emotions is seen in the faces of the men—some in pain, some stoic, others raring to go—all conveying the tension of the moment.

Pyle taught at the Drexel Institute of Art until 1900 when he left to open his own school for gifted students. He conducted stimulating, unregimented classes at Wilmington and, in the summer, at Chadd's Ford, Pennsylvania.

Seeking new challenges, Pyle accepted several commissions to paint murals. In an effort to master that art, he set sail for Europe in 1910 to study the Italian masterpieces. Unfortunately, Pyle died a year later in Florence, having completed only one mural.

"He Sang for Her as They Sat in the Gardens," illustration for Harper's Monthly, *April 1904. Collection of the Brandywine River Museum. Museum Purchase.*

"Courtship," cover illustration for The Ladies' Home Journal, *May 1897. Photo courtesy of Illustration House, Inc.*

"Mercy! Mercy! My Lord; cried poor Peter." Collection of the Society of Illustrators Museum of American Illustration.

"They Stood Staring at the Violent Sky," c. 1905. Collection of the Brandywine River Museum. Museum Purchase.

"The Nation Makers," 1903. Collection of the Brandywine River Museum. Purchased through a grant from the Mabel Pew Myrin Trust.

"A Wolf Had Not Been Seen in Salem For Thirty Years," illustration for Harper's Monthly, *December 1909. Delaware Art Museum, Howard Pyle Collection.*

"So the Treasure was Divided," from The Fate of Treasure Town, *by Howard Pyle, for* Harper's Monthly, *1905. Delaware Art Museum, Museum Purchase, 1912.*

"The Buccaneer was a Picturesque Fellow," from The Fate of Treasure Town, *by Howard Pyle, for* Harper's Monthly, *December 1905. Delaware Art Museum, Howard Pyle Collection. Museum Purchase, 1912.*

It was John P. Falter's goal as an artist to document the American way of life, from the Amish men of Pennsylvania to the cat fishermen of the Missouri River.

Born and raised in Nebraska, he enrolled at the Kansas City Art Institute in 1928, then in New York he studied at the Grand Central School of Art and got a scholarship to the Art Students League. He began illustrating for the pulps, and at age 20 sold his first magazine illustration to *Liberty*. He loved music as well as art and with his first earnings he bought a saxophone. Although a musical career did not materialize, he eventually painted 40 jazz greats from life, including Louis Armstrong, Jack Teagarden and Pee Wee Russell.

He became a successful illustrator of fiction and worked on many advertising accounts, notable among them a series for Pall Mall cigarettes. He entered the Navy in 1943, was commissioned a Lieutenant on special art assignments, and did more than 300 recruiting pamphlets and posters. While still in the Navy, he painted a series of 12 portraits of Great War Heroes, with text by Paul Gallico, which were published as *Esquire* gatefolds.

Falter's first *Saturday Evening Post* cover, "Gramercy Park," was published in 1944. There followed a series of paintings of famous streets in cities across the country. He produced about 200 covers for the *Post* until the magazine ceased publication in the early 1960s. He maintained a simple palette and never overworked his paintings. His strength lay in his wealth of ideas and his ability to create pictures that everyone could identify with. The *Post* cover on the facing page is typical of the wonderful human interest touches he introduced in so many of his pictures.

Falter also illustrated over 40 books for *Reader's Digest*, painted many portraits of celebrities, and in 1976 did a series of six Bicentennial paintings of historical subjects for the 3M Company.

"Schlitz—The Beer That Made Milwaukee Famous," full-page advertisement published in The Saturday Evening Post, 1951. The Charles Martignette Collection.

"Bedtime Prayers," illustration for Reader's Digest, 1966. Collection of the Society of Illustrators Museum of American Illustration.

"Drive-in Theatre," illustration for The Saturday Evening Post, *1961. Photo courtesy of Illustration House, Inc.*

(1 8 3 6 - 1 9 1 0)

Winslow Homer's career as an illustrator was of relatively short duration—from 1860 to 1875—but his painting career continued until his death in 1910. The distinction between "fine art" and "commercial art" scarcely existed at that time and many artists pursued simultaneous careers in painting for print and for galleries. Homer was an example of one who could achieve great success in both fields.

Born in Boston of old Yankee stock, Homer acquired drawing skills early in life under the influence of his mother,

an amateur watercolorist. He was apprenticed at 19 to a Boston lithographer and left two years later to begin freelancing. Encouraged by the work he was getting from *Harper's Weekly* and *Frank Leslie's Illustrated Newspaper*, Homer moved to New York in 1859.

Early in 1861 *Harper's* sent him to Washington to cover Lincoln's inauguration and later that year, as an artist-correspondent, to cover the Civil War. During the next four years he produced powerful drawings and paintings of the effect the conflict had on soldiers' lives. He worked with great directness and vigor, displaying his extraordinay skills. In contrast to the harshness of his experiences and depictions of war, Homer also had a gift for capturing the essence of peaceful rural and rustic

life, as evident in the pictures on these pages of children harvesting corn, picking berries and playing Snap the Whip.

An experienced hunter and fisherman, Homer loved the outdoor life. His early oils were authentic and direct illustrations of farm and summer resort scenes. In 1873 he took up watercolor. On a trip to England in 1881 he began painting the sea and fishermen, and two years later settled in Prout's Neck, Maine, where he lived alone in a studio facing the sea. He became the greatest painter of outdoor America—the forests, the mountains, and a series of the finest modern paintings of the sea. His summer visits to Cuba, Florida, Nassau and Bermuda resulted in brilliant and powerful watercolors and his most famous painting, "The Gulf Stream."

An 1862 full-color study of a Yankee sharpshooter stationed in a tree near Yorktown was run as a black-and-white line cut in several periodicals of the day. Private collection.

"Gathering Berries." Collection of Mr. and Mrs. Robert Crozier.

Photo courtesy of the Society of Illustrators Archives.

"The Last Days of Harvest." Collection of Mr. and Mrs. Robert Crozier.

(1 8 8 4 - 1 9 5 2)

Not only was Harvey Dunn a large, powerful man physically — he was also a "giant" in the field of illustration. He was a magnificent life force, a transcendental thinker and a great teacher. Through him, students had a direct line to the great painters of the past. Dunn considered teaching his most important work.

Dean Cornwell was perhaps Dunn's most famous student and one of the first to meet in the old Leonia, New Jersey, farmhouse where, in 1915, Dunn and Charles Chapman set up what came to be known as The Dunn School of Illustration.

To this school Dunn brought the philosophy of his own famous teacher, Howard Pyle.

While both Pyle and Dunn produced heroic illustrations, they differed somewhat in how they applied paint to canvas. Dunn's brush strokes seem to have been applied in haste, as though he could not wait to move on to the next challenge, whereas Pyle painted more meticulously, paying great attention to detail. On the facing page is a fine example of Dunn's use of muted color and his flair for the dramatic.

When Dunn was 17 he left the homestead in South Dakota, where he had grown up, to pursue an art career. He attended the Art Institute of Chicago from 1902 to 1904, then went to

Wilmington, Delaware, to study under Howard Pyle. After two years Pyle suggested that Dunn get a studio somewhere and see if he could get some work. Of course, Dunn succeeded in doing both. A great wave of advertising was then sweeping the country and advertisers were just beginning to realize that the weekly and monthly periodicals offered a great showcase for their products. Dunn was kept busy illustrating for them.

During World War I, Dunn was commissioned a Captain as an official war correspondent with the A.E.F. He lived in the trenches and went over the top with the men. His drawings and paintings of those experiences are now part of the Smithsonian Institution archives in Washington, D.C.

"Spring Planting," cover illustration for Country Gentleman, *January 28, 1922. Collection of Alan Goffman.*

"Storming the Bastille," published as endpapers for A Tale of Two Cities, *1921. Collection of the Society of Illustrators Museum of American Illustration.*

"Coal Miner," cover illustration for American Legion Monthly, *August 1932. Photo courtesy of Illustration House, Inc.*

"The Source," illustration for The Saturday Evening Post, *September 1, 1917. Collection of the Society of Illustrators Museum of American Illustration.*

"The Gray Dawn," illustration for The Saturday Evening Post, *1915. Photo courtesy of Illustration House, Inc.*

R O B E R T   P E A K

(1 9 2 8 - 1 9 9 2)

One of the most imaginative and prolific illustrators of the 20th century, Robert Peak revolutionized advertising in the film industry and is considered the "Father of the modern movie poster." The illustration on the facing page reveals how skillfully Peak was able to introduce multiple elements into a complicated design to create one stunning image. The exquisite Garbo, here surrounded by legendary superstars, is made even more glamorous by the brilliant white flashes emanating from her jeweled headdress. This is a technique Peak often used to create dazzling effects which added great excitement to his pictures.

Born in Denver, Colorado, Peak grew up in Kansas, attended Wichita State University, and after a stint in the military during the Korean War, went on to study at Art Center.

In 1953 Peak moved to New York, landed an Old Hickory Whiskey ad campaign, and from that point on his career skyrocketed. His work appeared in major advertising and national magazines. *Sports Illustrated* sent him on assignments throughout the world, including a safari to hunt ibex with the Shah of Iran.

United Artists hired Peak in 1961 to help promote "West Side Story." His innovative solution—painting characters and scenes into a single montage—became the first of over 100 such posters, among them "My Fair Lady," "Camelot," "Star Trek," "Equus" and "Apocalypse Now."

In 1961 Peak was named Artist of the Year by the Artists Guild of New York, and in 1977 the Society of Illustrators elected him to its Hall of Fame. For his 30 years of outstanding contribution to the film industry, he was presented the 1992 Key Art Lifetime Achievement Award by *The Hollywood Reporter.*

Peak's work is included in many permanent collections, and three of his paintings—of Anwar Sadat, Mother Teresa and Marlon Brando—hang in the Smithsonian Institution.

A glamorous figure, Peak lived a storybook life in Greenwich, Connecticut, with his family. After his wife of 28 years died, Peak moved to the West and spent his remaining years in Arizona and California.

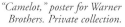

"Camelot," poster for Warner Brothers. Private collection.

Illustration for Good Housekeeping *magazine. Private collection.*

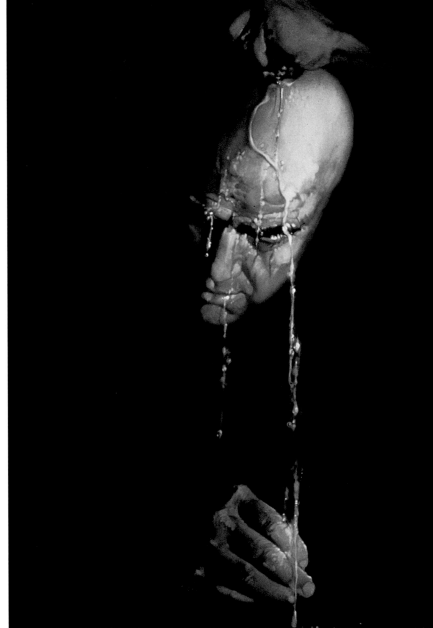

"Apocalypse Now," poster for Zoetrope Productions. Private collection.

Cover illustration for the Academy Players Directory 1981, *for the Academy of Motion Pictures Arts and Sciences. Private collection.*

"Funny Girl," poster for Warner Brothers. Private collection.

"Man of the Year," portrait of King Faisal for Time *magazine cover © 1975 Time Inc. Private collection.*

"Robert Henri." Private collection.

"Rollerball," poster for United Artists. Private collection.

Jack Nicholson in "Missouri Breaks," for United Artists. Private collection.

At the turn of the century, Wallace Morgan was working as a newspaper artist, traveling with reporters to cover train wrecks, coronations, strikes and murders, much as photographers do today. It required drawing on the spot, under pressure—excellent training which thereafter enabled him to draw without the need for models.

Born in New York City, Morgan attended classes at the National Academy for six years. While still in his twenties he worked as a staff artist on several New York newspapers, including *The Sun*, *The Herald* and *The Telegram*. In 1905 he was given a special Sunday feature in the Sunday *Herald* called "Fluffy Ruffles," the first series of its kind—a continuing cartoon story—which ran for three years and brought Morgan to the attention of magazine editors. He received his first magazine commission from *Collier's* and continued working for them for several years.

Some of Morgan's most interesting work was done in collaboration with Julian Street. They traveled across the country, Morgan sketching while Street wrote "Abroad at Home," a serial which ran in *Collier's*, and was then published by The Century Company in 1913. Other series by Street and Morgan appeared in *Everybody's Magazine*. The special flavor of his style made him a natural for illustrating the P.G. Wodehouse stories which ran in *The Saturday Evening Post*.

His art depicted the human condition with warmth and humor, as in the picture on the facing page. Here his subject gazes into a mirror, pondering his own importance. Morgan never labored over a drawing—if he ran into trouble he would abandon it and start anew. His early training as a newspaper artist contributed to his inimitable spontaneous style, as did his service during World War I where, as an official artist of the Expeditionary Forces he documented battles, top brass and life at the front lines.

"Poster Cat Stories." Collection of the Society of Illustrators Museum of American Illustration.

"The Little Warrior," April 19, 1920. Collection of the Society of Illustrators Museum of American Illustration.

Collection of the Society of Illustrators Museum of American Illustration.

"Harlem Nightclub," 1929. Collection of the Society of Illustrators Museum of American Illustration.

Collection of the Society of Illustrators Museum of American Illustration.

J . C . L E Y E N D E C K E R

(1 8 7 4 - 1 9 5 1)

In private life, Joseph Christian Leyendecker was a withdrawn, solitary individual, but his paintings quickly caught the attention of the public as well as clients, and he became one of the most highly acclaimed illustrators in history. Born in Germany, Leyendecker came to America with his family in 1882 and settled in Chicago. At age 16 he apprenticed at an engraving shop and after work attended classes at the Art Institute of Chicago. By 1896 he had saved enough so that he and his brother Frank, also an artist, could embark for Paris to study at the Academie Julian. Upon their return to Chicago two years later, J.C. found advertisers and publishers eager for his work, and within two years, felt ready to take on New York.

He painted his first cover for *The Saturday Evening Post* in 1899 and during the next 40 years produced 320 more for them. Leyendecker finished his covers months in advance of publication. His annual Easter covers usually featured blooms but were executed in the middle of winter, so sketches of flowers in his garden had to be made during the previous spring. The illustration on the facing page is typical of his skill in portraying beautiful people with radiant complexions, dressed in shimmering fabrics. His highly stylized way of painting with very wide, deliberate brush strokes became legendary.

In 1905 he received his most lucrative assignment—one which would continue for 25 years. The manufacturers of Arrow collars gave him carte blanche to create the prototype of a handsome, debonair gentleman for their advertising campaign. The "Arrow Collar Man" became a star overnight and in one month alone received 17,000 fan letters, gifts, marriage proposals and threats of suicide.

With Leyendecker's financial success came the freedom to live in luxury. In 1914 he built a 14-room mansion resembling a French chateau in New Rochelle, New York. By the end of the 1930s however, his popularity began to wane and he could no longer maintain his lavish lifestyle. At the age of 77 Leyendecker died suddenly from a heart attack.

"Weapons for Liberty," Third Liberty Loan Campaign poster for the U.S. Government, 1917. Collection of the Society of Illustrators Museum of American Illustration.

Cover illustration for Collier's *magazine, 1904. Collection of the Society of Illustrators Museum of American Illustration.*

Chesterfield cigarettes billboard, 1922. Collection of Tony D'Amico.

"Work for Victory," poster for World War I, 1917. Photo courtesy of Illustration House, Inc.

"Easter," cover illustration for The Saturday Evening Post, *March 31, 1934. Collection of the Society of Illustrators Museum of American Illustration.*

"Admiral Kirk," preliminary design, 1944. Collection of Mr. and Mrs. Gerald McConnell.

"Admiral Kirk Urges You to Buy More War Bonds," Timken Roller Bearing Company War Bond advertisement, 1944.

Kuppenheimer's Style Book for Fall/Winter 1917/1918. Collection of the Society of Illustrators Museum of American Illustration.

The Charles Martignette Collection.

Illustration for The Ladies' Home Journal, *1909. Collection of Mr. and Mrs. Gerald McConnell.*

"Uncle Sam," cover illustration for The Saturday Evening Post, *July 2, 1932. Photo courtesy of Illustration House, Inc.*

In the Depression years of the early thirties, Coburn M. Whitmore considered himself lucky to be working in the printing department of *McCall's* in Philadelphia. One day a distinguished gentleman in a tuxedo arrived to check on the color reproduction of his latest cover for *Redbook* magazine. The man was McClelland Barclay. That day may have been the turning point in Whitmore's life.

Born in Dayton, Ohio, Whitmore attended the Dayton Art Institute on a scholarship but had not decided on an art career until he met Barclay. So impressed was he with Barclay's lifestyle that he quit his job, borrowed $250 and moved to Chicago. There he apprenticed to Haddon Sundblom who, it turned out, had previously been an apprentice to Barclay. Sundblom persuaded Whitmore to enroll in evening classes at the Chicago Art Institute to study anatomy. After three years, Whitmore left Sundblom and went to work for the *Chicago Herald-Examiner* as a staff artist.

In the early 1940s Whitmore moved to New York and joined the Charles E. Cooper Studio. There he became a "star" at a time when "boy/girl" illustrations were immensely popular. For 30 years Whitmore's luscious women appeared on the covers and inside pages of *McCall's, The Ladies' Home Journal, Cosmopolitan* and *Good Housekeeping.* The women were all classy, beautifully dressed and very, very sexy—just the kind that readers thought every man wanted to meet and fall in love with. Although he most often portrayed the female, her male counterparts were equally attractive, handsome and debonaire types. A Whitmore illustration was always immediately recognizable by its air of high-style sophistication, elegance and good taste.

Whitmore lived the Good Life as graciously as he depicted it. A sports car enthusiast since his teens, he eventually raced a car of his own design at Sebring. In 1968 Whitmore moved his family to Hilton Head Island where he concentrated on painting portraits.

"Meet the Man and Marry Him," illustration for The Saturday Evening Post. *Collection of the Society of Illustrators Museum of American Illustration.*

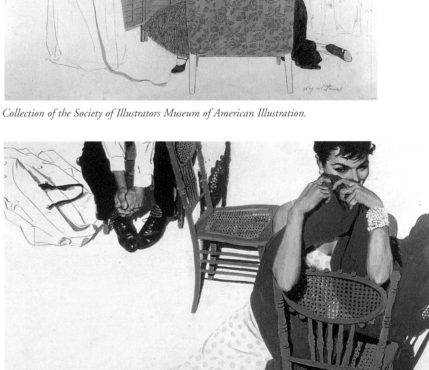

Collection of the Society of Illustrators Museum of American Illustration.

"Verna Vane," illustration for Cosmopolitan *magazine, 1942. The Charles Martignette Collection.*

Collection of the Society of Illustrators Museum of American Illustration.

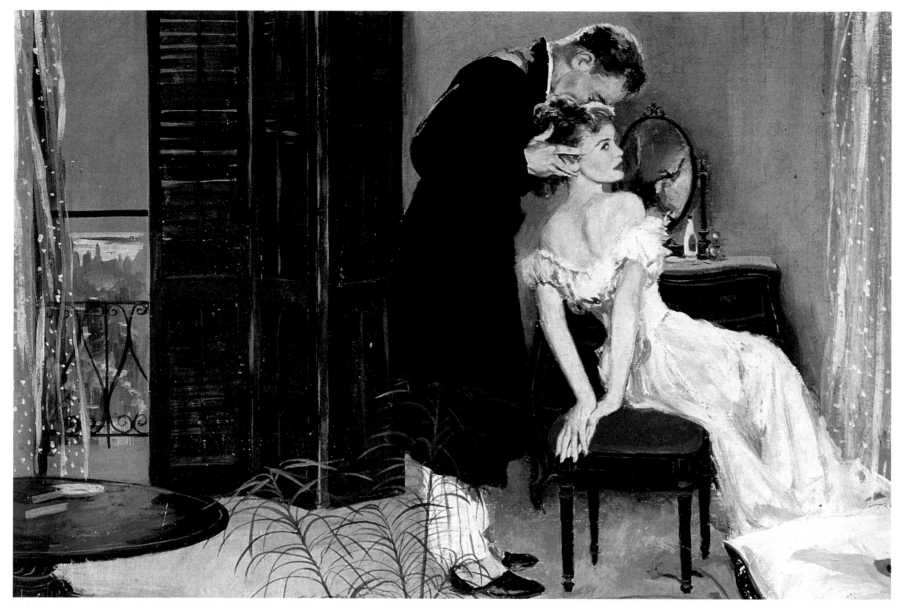

"The Years Between," September 1951. Collection of the Society of Illustrators Museum of American Illustration.

(1 8 7 7 - 1 9 5 1)

Intensely interested in historical subjects, Norman Mills Price restricted his work almost exclusively to that area. His painstaking research into every detail made each picture an authentic documentary. A traditional painter, he relished assignments that gave him an opportunity to create pictures with atmosphere and action. Some of his most successful illustrations were produced for a series of historical novels by Robert W. Chambers, one of which is shown on the facing page. In this scene a woman, dressed as an officer, surprises a man on horseback, leading one to wonder where that chance encounter may lead.

Price was born in the small Ontario town of Brampton, near Toronto. As a boy he was introduced to the illustrator's art through magazines such as *Harper's*, *Scribner's* and *The Century*, which he and other Canadian art students anxiously awaited each month. In 1896, after one year at the Ontario School of Art, he took a job with Grip Litho while continuing art school at night.

Price was equally interested in a music career. By 1902, however, his ambition to be a concert pianist had not materialized, so he decided to continue his art studies in Europe. Price and three fellow artists arrived in London, studied briefly at Goldsmith Institute and the Westminster School of Art, then opened Carlton Studios. Dismayed by the pressures of clients and collections, Price left for Paris in 1909, where he studied with Jean Paul Laurens at the Academie Julian.

He returned to America in 1911 and opened a branch of Carlton Studios in the Flatiron Building in New York. After one year he left the studio and began illustrating for most of the popular magazines and major advertisers.

Price was Honorary President of the Society of Illustrators from 1948 to 1951. Because of his dedication to the maintenance of illustration history and his tireless work as its Curator, the Society named its library in his honor.

"Captain Death," illustration for Liberty *magazine, March 31, 1928. The Charles Martignette Collection.*

"Love and the Lieutenant," illustration for Woman's Home Companion, *October 1934. Collection of the Society of Illustrators Museum of American Illustration.*

Photo courtesy of Illustration House, Inc.

"Love and the Lieutenant," illustration for Woman's Home Companion, *October 1934. Photo courtesy of Illustration House, Inc.*

FREDERIC REMINGTON

(1 8 6 1 - 1 9 0 9)

A robust and energetic individualist, Frederic Sackrider Remington was as much at home on the Western frontier as he was socializing with artists, publishers and writers in the East. His father, a Civil War hero and newspaper publisher, spent many hours on horseback with his son, who became an accomplished rider at a young age. These early experiences were the beginning of Remington's lifelong fascination with horses. He gained tremendous insight into their characteristics and behavior, and his knowledge of their anatomy enabled him to draw and paint them with great authenticity throughout his lifetime. Equal care and attention was given to the accuracy of locale and costume in his Western paintings.

Born in Canton, New York, Remington went to military school, then briefly to Yale. His interest in drawing and sports always took precedence over academic work. Lured by romantic tales of adventure, he took off for the West in 1881 to seek his fortune. He worked at various jobs, from herding cattle to raising sheep. Instead of riches, however, he returned from Montana with a sack full of drawings, one of which he sold to *Harper's Weekly*. Realizing that the Old West was rapidly changing, he returned to it again and again, determined to capture and document it before it disappeared.

In 1886 Remington's work appeared in *Harper's Weekly*, *St. Nicholas* and *Outing* in quick succession, followed by assignments from all the other major magazines. He delighted the American public with his work until 1903, when he turned to painting for exhibition. In 1898 he discovered sculpture and was virtually the first artist in America to use the lost wax process.

Remington went to Cuba as an artist-reporter to cover the Spanish-American War where he met and developed a lifelong friendship with Teddy Roosevelt. When Remington died of appendicitis at the age of 48, Roosevelt eulogized "The soldier, the cowboy and rancher, the Indian, the horse and cattle of the plains will live in his pictures, I verily believe, for all time."

"They Were a Hard Looking Set," 1887. Collection of the Brandywine River Museum. Gift of Catherine Auchincloss.

"Advance of Russian Infantry," illustration for Harper's Monthly, *April 1893.*

Collection of Amon Carter Museum, Fort Worth, Texas.

"The Canadian Mounted Police." Collection of the Brandywine River Museum. Museum Purchase.

As a youngster Benjamin Albert Stahl spent many hours in the Chicago Art Institute with his grandmother. Thanks to her encouragement, he developed an interest in art and at 17 got a job as an apprentice in an art studio. Five years later he joined Stevens, Sundblom and Stults as an artist.

In 1937 Stahl's work caught the eye of a *Saturday Evening Post* editor, who commissioned him to illustrate a story. Over the next 30 years Stahl painted more than 700 pictures for the *Post*, including the famous series for C.S. Forester's "Captain Horatio Hornblower."

Stahl left Chicago in 1943 and settled in Westport, Connecticut, where he was one of the founding faculty members of the Famous Artists Schools. He was kept busy illustrating for many magazines and national advertising campaigns. His strong compositions and superb draftsmanship are evident in all his paintings, but he was particularly admired for his more open form of painting. He claimed he was never one for fine detail and said he wanted his work to "excite the senses...to trigger an emotional response." And that it did.

Stahl wrote and illustrated a book, *Blackbeard's Ghost*, which Disney later made into a movie. He also painted six religious works to promote "Ben Hur" for MGM. A pioneer in television art instruction, Stahl produced "Journey into Art," an educational series.

In 1955 Stahl was commissioned by the Catholic Press to paint the Stations of the Cross. One of his most ambitious undertakings began ten years later when he decided to paint the same scenes again, but on a larger scale. He completed 15 murals, each 6 by 9 feet, and designed a building in Sarasota, Florida, in which to house them. In 1969 the uninsured paintings, valued at more than $1 million, were stolen from the Museum of the Cross and never recovered. Disheartened, Stahl moved to Mexico in 1972, but because of health problems eventually returned to Sarasota.

"Seated Girl with Flowers," 1970. Collection of the Society of Illustrators Museum of American Illustration.

"Commodore Hornblower," illustration for The Saturday Evening Post, 1946. Photo courtesy of Illustration House, Inc.

"She Turned a Wilderness into Home," sketch for John Hancock Life Insurance advertisement. Collection of the Society of Illustrators Museum of American Illustration.

"A Phony Story," 1941. Collection of the Society of Illustrators Museum of American Illustration.

"The Grand Reflector," illustration for The Saturday Evening Post. *Photo courtesy of Illustration House, Inc.*

E D W I N   A U S T I N   A B B E Y

(1 8 5 2 - 1 9 1 1)

The brilliant draftsmanship of Edwin Austin Abbey's pen-and-ink drawings were perfectly suited to the reproduction techniques of the late 1800s. His genius as an artist was further established when he began working in other media as well—watercolor, oil, pastel—and swiftly mastered them all. The delicately rendered, charming portrait on the facing page attests to his great skill in handling pastel.

A major contributor to the "Golden Age of American Illustration," Abbey was held in high esteem by art establishments on both sides of the Atlantic. Living in England as an American expatriate, he became a full member of the Royal Academy, painted the coronation of King Edward VII at the King's request, but declined an offer of knighthood in order to retain his U.S. citizenship.

Growing up in Philadelphia, Abbey attended the Pennsylvania Academy of Fine Arts and began illustrating books and magazines at the age of 16. At 19 he joined the staff at *Harper's*, concentrating on English scenes and Shakespearean works. A trip abroad in 1871 made him realize that England was a great source for authentic props, costumes, and backgrounds for his historical illustrations. He returned there seven years later to take up permanent residence.

Even his enormous murals for the Boston Public Library and the State Capitol in Harrisburg, Pennsylvania, were painted in England. The Capitol murals, for which he was paid $25 per square foot, are now valued at well over a million dollars.

In 1889 Abbey married a socialite and at their summer home in Gloucestershire they entertained such notables as Charles Dana Gibson, Augustus St. Gaudens, Stanford White, Henry James, James McNeill Whistler, Mark Twain and Arthur Conan Doyle. John Singer Sargent, a close friend, often used Abbey's Chelsea Lodge studio in London.

Abbey died in London in 1911, leaving behind an unfinished mural and a large collection of exquisite pen-and-ink illustrations. Today the Yale University Art Gallery in New Haven maintains the world's largest repository of Abbey's works.

Edwin Austin Abbey Memorial Collection, Yale University Art Gallery.

"The Quiet Life," 1887. Photo courtesy of the Archives of the American Illustrators Gallery, New York City.

"The Not Brown Mande." Collection of the Society of Illustrators Museum of American Illustration.

"Seated Woman in a Pink Dress," c. 1939. Photo courtesy of the Archives of the American Illustrators Gallery, New York City.

At a time when women were the exception in the illustration profession, Lorraine Fox created a special niche for herself. Her charming, imaginative pictures captivated readers of the popular magazines who published her work. The illustration shown opposite displays her neat, clean painting style and her skill at conveying an air of mystery to entice the reader. Her montage of a young sleuth, hot on the trail of a murder, is cleverly superimposed on a silhouette of Sherlock Holmes. A few clues, such as the bright red spinning top and large diamond, serve not only to further intrigue the viewer, but add interesting elements to the composition.

Born in Brooklyn of second generation German and Irish parents, Fox's artistic talent became apparent when she was quite young. Her grandmother instilled in her a fondness for nostalgia which was reflected in her early work, and her cartoonist brother's humor must have added a light touch to her style.

Fox graduated from Pratt Institute in 1944 and began working in the layout departments of various New York advertising agencies. In 1947 she did her first magazine illustration for *Better Homes and Gardens*; assignments from *Woman's Day*, *Good Housekeeping*, *Cosmopolitan*, *The Ladies' Home Journal*, *Redbook* and *McCall's* soon followed.

While at Pratt, Fox had met Bernard D'Andrea, an equally accomplished illustrator, and in 1951 they were married. In the mid-'50s, Fox joined D'Andrea at the Charles E. Cooper Studio, where the most prestigious group of illustrators at the time were working. In that rarified atmosphere of super talents she further developed her own unique style. In 1961 she enrolled in Ruben Tam's painting class at the Brooklyn Museum Art School and her four years of study there also had a great impact on her work

Fox taught at the Parsons School of Design and was a faculty member of the Famous Artists Schools in Westport, Connecticut. Her untimely death at age 54 came at a point in her career when she was painting some of her most interesting work.

"Wheelchair at the Beach," illustration for Reader's Digest. *Collection of the Society of Illustrators Museum of American Illustration.*

"Young Archeologist," illustration for Seventeen *magazine, 1971. Collection of the Society of Illustrators Museum of American Illustration.*

"Garden Fantasy," 1972. Collection of the Society of Illustrators Museum of American Illustration.

"Young Sleuth," illustration for Boys' Life *magazine, 1975. Collection of the Society of Illustrators Museum of American Illustration.*

Hard work was the key to success for the immigrant families living on the lower East side of New York City where Saul Tepper was born. He was no exception. As a youngster he won a correspondence course in the Landon School of Art, and at 19 was working full time as a letterer while attending art school at night. He studied at the Art Students League under George Bridgman, at the Grand Central School of Art under Harvey Dunn, and took composition classes at Cooper Union.

Dunn's teaching had a very strong influence on Tepper's way of thinking about composing his illustrations. Tepper also admired the way another great illustrator, Dean Cornwell, applied paint to canvas. The large painting on the opposite page, with its strong composition and dramatic lighting, is an example of the powerful images Tepper was able to create. He also had a marvelous way of painting into wet paint, making edges which could be achieved only by such a technique.

In 1925, he sold his first work to a major magazine—*Liberty* bought one of his samples and created a story around the picture. Shortly thereafter, *Collier's*, *The Ladies' Home Journal*, *The Saturday Evening Post* and *Country Gentleman* commissioned him to do story illustrations. *Woman's Home Companion*, *American*, *Cosmopolitan* and *Good Housekeeping* were not far behind. By the 1930s Tepper's work commanded top dollar. Advertising campaigns for Chesterfield cigarettes and General Electric followed, as well as many other national accounts, such as Mobil Oil, Texaco, Packard and Coca-Cola.

Tepper also taught and lectured at Pratt Institute and Cooper Union. His talent was not limited to illustration, however. He loved music and wrote many popular songs which were recorded by Nat King Cole, Ella Fitzgerald, Glenn Miller, Harry James and other such performers. In the 1950s Tepper got involved in creating images for TV commercials. He became a television art director for the J. Walter Thompson and the BBDO advertising agencies. In his final years Tepper devoted himself to restoring his paintings and inventing tools for that process.

"Boys Visiting Pawnshop," illustration for The Saturday Evening Post, *1928. Collection of the Society of Illustrators Museum of American Illustration. On loan from Joan Anton.*

"Star Magic," illustration for American *magazine. Collection of the Society of Illustrators Museum of American Illustration. On loan from Joan Anton.*

"Baggage Section B," Chesterfield cigarettes advertisement for Liggett & Meyers. Collection of the Society of Illustrators Museum of American Illustration.

"Behold the Vine Was Before Me," illustration for The Delineator *magazine, 1934. Photo courtesy of Illustration House, Inc.*

HOWARD CHANDLER CHRISTY

(1 8 7 3 - 1 9 5 2)

The poised, elegant female in the painting on the facing page has all the qualities that made Howard Chandler Christy's art so memorable. Swathed in furs and feathers she is the epitome of the fashionably dressed woman of that period. Her beautifully drawn, delicate hands reveal that they were never exposed to the harsher indignities of life. Less reserved are the nymphets which adorn the walls of the Cafe des Artistes in New York City, where Christy's murals have thrilled diners since the 1930s.

Although best known for his luscious "Christy Girls," his first commercial assignment, at age 10, was to paint a bull for the local butcher shop in Duncan Falls, Ohio, where he grew up.

At 19 Christy left for New York to study under William Merritt Chase at the Art Students League. Always strapped for money, Christy sold a sketch to *Life* magazine for six dollars, and realized that he had to enter the commercial arena in order to survive.

In 1898, commissioned by *Leslie's Weekly* and *Scribner's* to cover the Spanish American War, Christy's illustrations received wide circulation. En route to Cuba he met Teddy Roosevelt and did a portfolio of sketches of the Rough Riders which was published as a book. By the time Christy returned home he was celebrated as a military artist.

Tired of depicting war, when assigned to illustrate "The Soldier's Dream," Christy portrayed a beautiful woman in the smoke of an infantryman's pipe. So popular did this picture become that the "Christy Girl" was born. Versions of this modern American woman filled magazines, ads and posters everywhere.

Christy went on to write and illustrate books, paint portraits of celebrities, including royalty, and in 1939 began a huge mural of "The Signing of the Constitution" for the Capitol Building in Washington, D.C., his first of many historical murals. Upon his death in 1952 he left behind an unfinished portrait of General Douglas MacArthur and plans for an historic painting of Gettysburg.

"For Thine is the Kingdom and the Power and the Glory Forever." Collection of Alan Goffman.

"Bill of Rights" poster. Photo courtesy of Illustration House, Inc.

Magazine cover, 1912. The Charles Martignette Collection.

"Americans All" poster. Collection of Alan Goffman.

"Last of the Mohicans," 1913. The Charles Martignette Collection.

Portrait of Nancy Palmer Christy, 1923. Photo courtesy of the Archives of the American Illustrators Gallery, New York City.

*"The Golf Links," 1902.
The Charles Martignette
Collection.*

*"Peek-a-Boo," 1933.
The Charles
Martignette Collection.*

*"Garden of Eden," 1925. The
Charles Martignette Collection.*

*"Cafe des Artistes Nude,"
1925. The Charles
Martignette Collection.*

*"I'd Join the Navy" poster.
Collection of the Society of
Illustrators Museum of
American Illustration.*

*"Fight or Buy Bonds"
poster. Collection of the
Society of Illustrators
Museum of American
Illustration.*

By painting portraits and drawing caricatures of the rich and famous in the social, artistic, political, and literary circles of the early 1900s, James Montgomery Flagg himself attained celebrity status. He became universally recognized when his "I Want You" recruiting posters appeared during World Wars I and II.

A native New Yorker, Flagg attended the Art Students League, and by the age of 16 was contributing humorous drawings to *Life*, *Judge*, and *St. Nicholas* magazines. In 1898 he went to England for further study and while there his first book,

Yankee Girls Abroad, was published. These fashionable beauties became the forerunners of the famous "Flagg Girl."

The following year Flagg married a socialite and together they traveled throughout Europe. Returning to New York in 1904 they moved into a studio/apartment on West 67th Street where Flagg began turning out illustrations at the rate of one a day. For many years he illustrated the "Jeeves" series by P.G. Wodehouse in *Collier's* which, along with the many other magazines he worked for, helped make him the highest paid illustrator of his day.

Although Flagg's favorite medium was pen-and-ink, he was equally talented with the brush. The illustration on the facing page shows how ably he depicted a scene with a few deft strokes

of the watercolor brush. The handsome couple is caught in an amusing situation and the woman, obviously enjoying the poor chap's embarrassment, is delightful.

Flagg was also a poet and satirist, wrote a syndicated column and a Broadway play, wrote and acted in 24 short screenplays, and produced a number of the Society of Illustrators' amateur productions.

The period between World War I and II found Flagg hobnobbing with the Barrymores, the Roosevelts, and Hollywood starlets. A flamboyant individual, he made headlines with his outrageous escapades in New York. In later years, failing eyesight forced him to abandon his art, and after two heart attacks Flagg died in 1960 at the age of 82.

"Her Steady," cover illustration for Judge *magazine, August 8, 1914. The Charles Martignette Collection.*

Magazine story illustration, c. 1915. The Charles Martignette Collection.

"And the World Moved on, Forgotten," illustration for Liberty *magazine. Collection of Everett Raymond Kinstler.*

"The Fencer," 1938. Collection of the Lotos Club, New York.

"Kiss and Make Up," illustration for Judge *magazine. Photo courtesy of Illustration House, Inc.*

Story illustration. The Charles Martignette Collection.

Story illustration. The Charles Martignette Collection.

Inside illustration for Cosmopolitan, *1925.*

Cover illustration for Life *magazine, 1910. Collection of Everett Raymond Kinstler.*

Story illustration. The Charles Martignette Collection.

"Standing Nude." Collection of the Lotos Club, New York.

Cover illustration for women's magazine, 1930. The Charles Martignette Collection.

Cover illustration for Life magazine, 1909. The Charles Martignette Collection.

105

Although an artistic career was what Stanley W. Galli aspired to even as a youngster, the lean years of the Depression in the 1930s forced him to take on many odd jobs in order to survive. He fried doughnuts as a baker's apprentice, worked as a ranch hand in Nevada and a longshoreman in San Francisco, his birthplace. After saving enough money he enrolled at the California School of Fine Arts.

A San Francisco art service hired him out of school and he later became a partner in the firm. In 1942 the Navy Department called him into special service to work at structuring educational programs. After the war Galli returned to his firm but found the demands of business getting in the way of his first love—drawing. He left the partnership and devoted himself to illustrating,

Galli's first big break on the national scene came from Weyerhaeuser, who commissioned him to create a new image for the company based on themes of conservation. Galli made over 50 paintings himself and enlisted other artists to illustrate wildlife scenes. The campaign was so effective it remained a key factor in the company's advertising program for over 14 years. Galli's ad on the facing page is typical of the conservation theme of the Weyerhaeuser campaign. His style is based on good draftsmanship and strong contrast between light and dark, with details intricately drawn out in the light areas. He also designed 26 stamps for the U.S. Postal Service, mostly commemoratives for wildlife conservation.

Assignments from the East began flowing in—from *The Saturday Evening Post*, *True*, *McCall's*, *Today's Woman* and *Reader's Digest*.

Galli, dividing his time between his home in Kentfield, California, and his studio in Tuscany, Italy, eventually shifted the emphasis of his work from illustration to easel paintings of the vanished past of Colonial Spanish California.

"The Gift of Deer," sketch for Reader's Digest Condensed Books. *Collection of the Society of Illustrators Museum of American Illustration.*

Photo courtesy of Illustration House, Inc.

Illustration for Weyerhaeuser Paper Co. advertisement. Collection of the Society of Illustrators Museum of American Illustration.

"Doctor Blanke's First Command," illustration for The Saturday Evening Post, *1961. Collection of the Society of Illustrators Museum of American Illustration.*

"Storm," illustration for Weyerhaeuser Paper Co. advertisement, c. 1950s. Collection of the Society of Illustrators Museum of American Illustration.

The ultimate compliment for Frederic Rodrigo Gruger was the praise he received from authors whose stories he illustrated. Fannie Hurst, for instance, wrote "You have said in your drawings what I tried to say in 100,000 words. I am your debtor!"

A native of Philadelphia, Gruger studied at the Pennsylvania Academy. Like many of his contemporaries, he became enamored with the pen-and-ink drawings of artists such as Edwin Austin Abbey, and it was with that medium that he began his career as a newspaper artist. During the 1890s his on-the-spot drawings of fires, a presidential inauguration and the America's Cup Race brought immediacy and excitement to the pages of the *Philadelphia Ledger.*

Gruger began working for *The Saturday Evening Post* in 1898, and in the course of the next 45 years produced over 2,700 illustrations for them. In the early 1920s, he was illustrating the stories of hundreds of authors, including Theodore Dreiser, Edith Wharton, Agatha Christie, William Faulkner, Ring Lardner, Sinclair Lewis, F. Scott Fitzgerald and other great writers whose literary outpourings filled the pages of the popular magazines.

In his illustration for "The Captives" pictured here, Gruger portrayed the terrified emotions of the captured people with great sensitivity. While he paid great attention to detail in all his pictures, it was his inspired interpretation of the drama taking place that made his work so outstanding.

Although Gruger's earliest illustrations were done in pen-and-ink, his later medium of choice was the Wolff pencil. He worked on inexpensive cardboard used by newspapers for mounting silver prints. It was soon manufactured under his name and became known as Gruger Board. By the mid-1930s, demand for his work was on the wane. He had not made the transition from black-and-white illustration to color. Close-up "boy/girl" illustrations were "in," and his detailed pictorial approach was no longer in vogue.

Book illustration for The Thunderer. *Collection of the Society of Illustrators Museum of American Illustration.*

"True Thomas," illustration for Good Housekeeping *magazine, March 1926. Photo courtesy of Illustration House, Inc.*

"The Captives." Two separate illustrations for a double-page spread in The Saturday Evening Post, *February 13, 1937. Collection of Mr. and Mrs. Albert Gold. Photo courtesy of Illustration House, Inc.*

J O H N   G A N N A M

(1 9 0 7 - 1 9 6 5)

Asuperb watercolorist, John Gannam's genius was the envy of many artists who undertook working in that challenging medium. His perfectionism, however, was known to drive art directors to despair. He worked on his paintings over and over again, regardless of deadlines, until he achieved what he considered a satisfactory solution.

His mastery of watercolor is evident in the picture on the facing page, one of a series of delightful ads that he illustrated for a Pacific Mills campaign. How he handled the various

fabrics—from the transparency of the woman's gown to the fluffy, rumpled bedsheets—is remarkable. With soft pastel colors and high key lighting he imparted a feeling of serenity, comfort and luxury.

Born in Lebanon, Gannam grew up in Chicago. On his way to school each day he became fascinated by an exhibition of Frederic Remington's illustrations in a bookshop window. The seed was planted. When Gannam was 14 his father died so he quit school to become the family's breadwinner. While working at the Blackstone Hotel he enrolled at the Chicago Academy of Fine Arts but had to leave after two weeks because his long working hours left him too exhausted to study. There followed four years of various menial jobs, then an opportunity

arose in a fashion studio where he acquired enough drawing skills to venture out as a freelancer, and finally, to work in Grauman's, a big-time Chicago studio. In 1926 he moved to Detroit to work in the Gray, Garfield & Ladriere studio, and four years later to New York, where he found a ready market for his work.

Some of Gannam's most memorable advertising campaigns for Pacific Mills and St. Mary's Blankets appeared in the 1940s. Later, he was kept busy illustrating for magazines such as *Collier's*, *Woman's Home Companion*, *Good Housekeeping*, *Cosmopolitan* and *The Ladies' Home Journal*. Whether it was a wet city street scene or a lovely woman in her boudoir, Gannam was able to evoke the mood and setting with great sensitivity

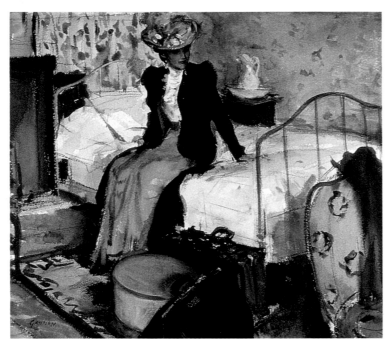

Illustration for McCall's *magazine, December 1938. Collection of the Society of Illustrators Museum of American Illustration.*

"First Show," illustration for Cosmopolitan *magazine. Photo courtesy of Illustration House, Inc.*

"Wagon Train Camp." Collection of the Society of Illustrators Museum of American Illustration.

Illustration for Pacific Mills advertisement. Photo courtesy of Illustration House, Inc.

(1 9 0 7 - 1 9 8 9)

Dedicated to accurately documenting the history of the American West, John Clymer based his information on family diaries, visits to actual sights of events and thorough research in museums. His paintings became authentic re-creations of history. Clymer, born in Ellensburg, Washington, was interested in art as a child, and took correspondence courses when he was 13. Two years later, his first painting appeared in the *Seattle Times*, and at 16 he sold some pen-and-ink illustrations to the Colt Firearms Company. After graduating from high school, Clymer moved to

Vancouver, Canada, where he worked as an illustrator for a mail-order house during the day, attended art school at night and after classes free-lanced and studied with George Southwell, who instructed him for three years at no charge. His days began at 8 a.m. and ended at 3:00 in the morning. Totally exhausted by the time he was 21, his doctor prescribed working outdoors, so Clymer took a job as a deck hand on a paddlewheeler delivering supplies to the Indians in the Yukon. With health restored, he moved to Toronto where he became a successful illustrator but, anxious to break into the New York market, he moved to Westport, Connecticut, in 1936.

He sold his first cover to *The Saturday Evening Post* in 1941, and painted over 100 more in the ensuing years. The magazine

wanted human interest stories, which were very popular with the reading public at that time. The serene landscape on the opposite page demonstrates how Clymer combined his love of nature, which dominated much of his work, with the human element.

After serving in the Marine Corps during World War II, Clymer began painting pictures of the Northwest, and as fast as he could paint them his gallery was selling them. He decided to devote his time entirely to painting the American West and in 1979 moved to Teton Village, Wyoming. Among the many awards Clymer garnered, was a gold medal from the Cowboy Artists of America.

Cover illustration for The Saturday Evening Post, *May 21, 1960. © 1960 by The Curtis Publishing Comany.*

"Glacier National Park," cover illustration for The Saturday Evening Post, *July 30, 1960. Photo courtesy of the Archives of the American Illustrators Gallery, New York City.*

"Mother and Cub," 1953. Collection of Mr. and Mrs. Gerald McConnell.

"Bass Fishing," cover illustration for The Saturday Evening Post, *June 13, 1959. Photo courtesy of the Archives of the American Illustrators Gallery, New York City.*

Illustrations of large groups of well-dressed people in elaborate settings revealed Henry Patrick Raleigh's talent for portraying the ultimate in fashionable society. Notable were the Maxwell House Coffee ads that he illustrated for years, which depicted the Southern Ante-Bellum elite in luxurious homes. Even in a canoe, as in the picture opposite, elegance was foremost, his characters dressed in formal attire. By the types of models, poses and clothes that he chose to illustrate, he accurately depicted the fashion and style trends of the wealthier classes of the day.

Raleigh was born in Portland, Oregon, and moved to San Francisco when he was 12. In order to help support his family he quit school and got a job as a shipping clerk. His boss, recognizing Raleigh's drawing skills, sent him to Hopkins Academy in San Francisco to study art for two years. At 17 he was hired by the *San Francisco Chronicle* as a reporter-artist to cover local newsworthy events. Later, he covered the Spanish-American War and the Klondike Gold Rush.

By the time he was 19 he was working for the *San Francisco Examiner* as one of their highest paid artists. His work attracted the attention of William Randolph Hearst, who sent him to New York to work on the *Journal*. Raleigh also did special features for the *New York World*, an experience which helped him break into the magazine field.

Working for publications such as *Vanity Fair*, *Harper's Bazaar* and *The Saturday Evening Post*, he became famous and wealthy enough to indulge his passion for the "good life"— yachts, travel, a home in Westport, Connecticut, and a studio in New York City's Gramercy Park. It was a lifestyle he thought would never end. However, unable to adapt to the new trends in the illustration market, and unwilling to accept the social mores of the late '30s and '40s, he grew morose and introverted. His spirit broken, in 1944 he took his own life.

Illustration for The Saturday Evening Post, *1931. The Charles Martignette Collection.*

"The Center of Attention," 1929. Collection of the Society of Illustrators Museum of American Illustration.

Photo courtesy of Illustration House, Inc.

Photo courtesy of Illustration House, Inc.

"A Dream Comes True," illustration for The Saturday Evening Post, *June 1928. The Charles Martignette Collection.*

"New Wine," illustration for The Saturday Evening Post, *1932. The Charles Martignette Collection.*

(1 8 9 1 - 1 9 5 8)

For over 35 years Carl Oscar August Erickson dominated the field of fashion illustration. He himself was the personification of the elegance and sophistication he depicted in his pictures. A true boulevardier, he wore a bowler hat and cornflower boutonniere, carried a walking stick and participated in the heady lifestyle of the international set.

Eric was born in Joliet, Illinois, of Swedish parents and at an early age showed more interest in drawing and boxing than in his schoolwork. For two years he attended the Chicago Academy of Fine Arts where he was dubbed "Eric," a name and signature by which he would ever after be known. Following art school he worked for the Marshall Field department store, and advertising agencies such as Lord & Thomas. He moved to New York City in 1914 where he continued illustrating for advertisers and produced fashion drawings for *Dry Goods Economist.*

In 1920 Eric made his first trip to Paris, the city which became his second home for the next 20 years. He illustrated for French publications and in 1923 began his long association with *Vogue* magazine as fashion illustrator, portraitist and reporter. Famous designers such as Mainbocher, Chanel, Schiaparelli, Dior and Yves St. Laurent vied to have Eric draw their creations. Because the world of fashion changes so drastically and at such a fast pace it seems incredible that the illustration on the facing page, which Eric painted many, many years ago, might very well have appeared in a current magazine. This delicate, lovely drawing of a sophisticated model reflects the innate good taste of the artist himself.

His portraits of celebrities such as Gertrude Stein, Colette, Edith Piaf, Toscanini and Franklin Roosevelt were equally in demand. He became known as the "Toulouse-Lautrec of America."

Eric returned to America in 1940, a few weeks after Hitler's occupation of France, and continued illustrating for *Vogue* until his death in 1958. In 1959, the Brooklyn Museum of Art held a retrospective exhibition of his work.

Collection of Arthur and Janet Weithas.

Fashion illustration. Photo courtesy of Illustration House, Inc.

Collection of Jack Potter.

Collection of Arthur and Janet Weithas.

Mark English's work has undergone several style changes over the years, but his superb design skills and use of subtle variations of color and value have prevailed throughout. The painting on the facing page is intriguing. One wonders what the mysterious piece of paper in the girl's hand may signify and what story lies behind the dream-like atmosphere of this picture.

A native of Hubbard, Texas, English's first job was picking cotton, but he worked his way out of the cotton fields by learning to paint signs. He chased rodeos, painting "Welcome Rodeo Fans" on store windows, painted billboards and, when drafted into the Army, painted signs for the Training Aid Section. English said from that point on "there was no place to go but up."

After his stint in the Army he attended Art Center College in Los Angeles. Before graduating in 1960, the N.W. Ayer advertising agency hired him for their Detroit office where he worked for two years as an art director on automotive accounts. He felt that experience helped him in later years, as an illustrator, to better understand the problems facing art directors. In 1964 English relocated to Redding, Connecticut, and quickly established himself as a leading magazine illustrator.

English's first editorial assignment came from *The Saturday Evening Post*, after which work began to flow in steadily from *The Ladies' Home Journal*, *Good Housekeeping*, *Sports Illustrated*, *Redbook*, *McCall's*, *Time*, and most major magazines.

In addition to the numerous awards that English received, he won the Society of Illustrators Hamilton King Award in 1967 and in 1969 was named "Artist of the Year" by the Artists Guild of New York. In 1977 an offer from Hallmark Cards to serve as artist-in-residence prompted a move to Kansas City, Missouri, where he conducted teaching sessions for Hallmark's staff artists. He also taught at the Kansas City Art Institute until 1987, when he left to concentrate on painting for galleries as well as his illustration career.

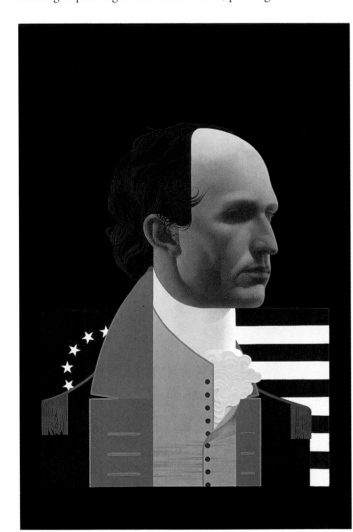

Poster of "George Rogers Clark," 1978. Collection of the National Park Services. Photo courtesy of the artist.

Much Ado About Nothing, *cover illustration for Bantam Books, 1983. Collection of the artist.*

Illustration for Redbook *magazine, April 7, 1982. Collection of the Society of Illustrators Museum of American Illustration.*

"American Indian," promotion for Mohawk Paper Company, 1989. Collection of the artist.

Cover illustration for Step-by-Step Graphics, *1988. Collection of the artist.*

Cover illustration for Eddie Bauer winter catalog, 1983. Collection of the artist.

Great Expectations, *cover illustration for Bantam Books, 1986. Collection of the artist.*

Cover illustration for Eddie Bauer winter catalog, 1993. Collection of the artist.

"Girl at Barn," story illustration for The Ladies' Home Journal, *1972. Collection of the artist.*

"Thomas Jefferson," portrait for the National Park Services, 1980. Collection of the artist.

Milton Caniff, in a tribute to his friend and fellow cartoonist Noel Sickles, wrote "This restless genius was the greatest natural cartoonist I ever knew." Sickles began his career as a cartoonist but went on to become one of the most highly regarded illustrators of black-and-white art. He also used color very effectively, working in both colored inks and gouache, but his superb drawings needed very little enhancement. In the picture on the facing page, the fact that his color range is quite limited merely adds to the starkness of the scene. Large masses of icy blue give emphasis to the sense of cold, and a touch of red in the hat draws the eye right to the subject.

Sickles grew up in Chillicothe, Ohio, where he watched his father draw pictures of his memories as a railroad man. His interest in art aroused, young Sickles took a correspondence course in cartooning from the Landon School of Art and haunted the library, studying the illustrations in books and publications. At the age of 19, he was hired as a political cartoonist by the *Ohio State Journal*. Three years later he began a cartoon strip, "Scorchy Smith," which became the ultimate model for adventure strips.

By 1940 Sickles had abandoned cartooning in order to begin his illustration career. With the advent of World War II, *Life* magazine commissioned him to depict events which could not be photographed. This resulted in a contract with both the War and Navy Departments for him to draw highly sensitive material.

Following the war, Sickles' work began appearing in the major magazines. *Life* sponsored an exhibition of his work that toured the world. In Cairo the exhibition was stolen and the originals, among them his dramatic drawings of Hemingway's *The Old Man and the Sea*, were lost forever. Fortunately, some of his best works are in the collections of the National Geographic Society and *Reader's Digest*.

"The Spy Who Changed His Mind," illustration for Reader's Digest, *May 1970. Collection of the Society of Illustrators Museum of American Illustration.*

"KGB: The Swallow's Nest," illustration for Reader's Digest, *August 1970. Collection of the Society of Illustrators Museum of American Illustration.*

"The Coffee House," illustration for Reader's Digest. *Collection of the Society of Illustrators Museum of American Illustration.*

"900 Days: The Siege of Leningrad," illustration for Reader's Digest, *April 1968.*
Collection of the Society of Illustrators Museum of American Illustration.

At the time that Franklin Booth was growing up on a farm in Indiana, most of the reproductions in books and magazines were printed from steel or wood engravings. Assuming that the fine lines he saw in the illustrations were drawn individually by hand, he painstakingly copied them, line for line, with pen and ink. Determined to become an artist, he practiced endlessly and eventually developed a unique line technique that served him well for the rest of his life.

Booth was educated at the Quaker Academy in Westfield, Indiana, and at age 25 was hired by the *Indianapolis News* as a writer and artist. A year later, feeling the need for more art training, he went to the Art Institute of Chicago. After four years of intensive study, he moved to New York City and found employment with *Munsey's Publications*.

In 1906 he went to Spain for a year of sketching and painting, after which he returned to New York and settled down to pursue his illustration career. His work began appearing in all the leading magazines and his career zoomed into national prominence. The feeling of space and lofty grandeur of the composition on the facing page is typical of Booth's work. He possessed a creative imagination which he applied to all his work, whether for an advertisement or an editorial assignment. His dexterity with the pen was masterful, as was his ability to achieve a full range of values by merely using black ink on white paper.

After long periods of working seven days and nights a week, he took periodic vacations—on one such occasion traveling throughout the United States in his chauffeur-driven Rolls Royce.

In the mid-1930s Booth taught at the Phoenix Art Institute, where he tried to open the minds of his students to the worlds of imagination, spirit, and emotions. Booth himself was interested in everything that went on in nature and had an artist's sheer instinct for beauty.

"Hall of Aisles." Collection of the Society of Illustrators Museum of American Illustration.

"Heroes of Yesterday," illustration for The Saturday Evening Post. *Collection of Mr. and Mrs. Gerald McConnell.*

Illustration for Everybody's Magazine, *September 1908. Photo courtesy of the Society of Illustrators Archives.*

Photo courtesy of Illustration House, Inc.

Neysa Moran McMein was a legend in her own time—a great artist and one of the most fabulous social figures in the 1920s and '30s. Her great friend Noel Coward was among a host of artistic, literary and theatrical celebrities who visited McMein at her studio in the Hotel des Artistes.

Born in Quincy, Illinois, McMein paid her way through the Art Institute of Chicago by writing music and playing the piano. Her first job as an artist was sketching hats for the Gage Brothers Department Store, then she joined a vaudeville troupe to write songs and music. The act folded, but she found herself in New York City, where she sold her first picture of a pretty girl for $75.

McMein illustrated her first cover for *The Saturday Evening Post* in 1915. Covers for *Woman's Home Companion, Collier's* and *McClure's* followed, as well as advertising assignments for clients such as Cadillac and Palmolive. Her pastel portraits showed women of intelligence and grace with a cool, commanding sense of self, unlike the baby-doll look that was fashionable at the time. A good example of her skill at portraying real women is shown in the portrait opposite. A feeling of well-being and self-confidence is conveyed in this picture of a fashionably dressed beauty. McMein was gifted in her use of pastels, a fairly difficult medium to conquer, and the way she blended her edges was truly exquisite.

In 1923 she painted her first cover for *McCall's* and from 1924 to 1936 she held an exclusive contract with that magazine to do their covers. When the contract expired, she turned to oil portraiture. President Warren Harding, Chief Justice Charles Evans Hughes and Charlie Chaplin sat for her, as well as the country's most prominent women, including Edna St. Vincent Millay and Katherine Cornell.

The Whitney Museum of American Art established a memorial fund in her honor which is used to purchase work by living American artists.

Advertisement for the custom built Cadillac-Fisher Bodies V-63 chassis, October 1924. Photo courtesy of Illustration House, Inc.

Cover illustration for Woman's Home Companion, *June 1938. The Charles Martignette Collection.*

"Seated Nude." Collection of the Society of Illustrators Museum of American Illustration.

"Deco Woman." Private collection.

JOHN LaGATTA

(1 8 9 4 - 1 9 7 7)

Noted for his exquisite paintings of women, John LaGatta had a unique talent for revealing the female figure beneath the clothing in a sensuous yet most circumspect manner. Two of the illustrations on these pages—the bathers opposite, and the woman in a yellow gown, below—are perfect examples of how neatly he achieved that effect. The women are elegant and provocative, and at the same time epitomize sex, glamour and sophistication. His focus was on the figure; backgrounds, if any, played a secondary role. An aura of romance pervaded much of his work and always, the element of good taste was in evidence.

LaGatta himself cut a glamorous figure and in his heyday was considered a celebrity, with an apartment and studio in New York, a house on Long Island and a farm near Woodstock.

Born in Naples, Italy, he came to America at an early age and at 14 enrolled at the New York School of Fine and Applied Art. He later attended Parsons and the Art Students League as well. Through much of the 1920s he worked primarily in advertising but finally became bored with drawing product-oriented situations. He closed his New York studio and moved to Woodstock for a year in order to develop a portfolio of illustrations concentrating on women. This experiment was so successful that in a very short time his work was used regularly by such publications as *Cosmopolitan, The Ladies' Home Journal* and *Redbook.*

During the following two decades he turned out work at breakneck speed to satisfy the great demand for his work. He was much sought after by both advertising and editorial clients and was one of the most prolific and highly paid illustrators of his day.

As World War II approached, however, the demand for romantic illustration waned. LaGatta, by then in poor health, moved to California, where he taught at Art Center and served on the faculty for 21 years until his death at the age of 83.

Collection of Arpi Ermoyan.

Photo courtesy of Illustration House, Inc.

Illustration for Cosmopolitan *magazine, August 1949. Collection of the Society of Illustrators Museum of American Illustration.*

"Up From the Sextette," illustration for The Saturday Evening Post, *January 1, 1934. The Charles Martignette Collection.*

"Lie if You Must," illustration for Redbook *magazine, August 1938. Collection of the Society of Illustrators Museum of American Illustration.*

"James McVane, M.D.," illustration for Redbook *magazine, April 1938. Collection of the Society of Illustrators Museum of American Illustration.*

Although he produced an enormous number of advertising illustrations over the years, it was in James W. Williamson's editorial work that his sense of humor emerged and became his most engaging characteristic. His uncomplicated style got the point across immediately. With a simple and direct approach, he distilled action and renderings down to their essentials, and the crisp, clean lines of his drawings often required no embellishment other than flat washes of color.

Born in Omaha, Nebraska, at an early age he became fascinated with Howard Pyle's pen technique, which he tried to copy. During his teens he continued to draw and was influenced by the work of Franklin Booth and Carl Erickson.

Williamson was a graduate of the 1923 class at Yale. While still in college, he sold his first work to the old *Life* magazine. There followed a series of ads for Kelly Springfield Tires that appeared in *Vanity Fair* and were so successful that the agency put him under contract to Ford Motor Company. At about the same time he began illustrating for *Woman's Home Companion*, *The Delineator*, *Judge* and nearly all the major magazines, including *The Saturday Evening Post*, where his work appeared for over 30 years.

In 1942 he became involved in a top secret mission for the war effort about which little is known, except that he trained in Canada, was smuggled out to spend a year in Istanbul, six months in Cairo and 15 months in Rome. He returned to New York in 1946 and to the advertising business where he was warmly received and given more work. Clients included Arrow Shirts, Clicquot Club Ginger Ale, Paul Jones and Yardley, to name a few.

Fed up with the cold winters, Williamson moved to a suburb of San Juan, Puerto Rico, in 1952 where he continued to work and enjoy life.

"There's no Mayonnaise in Ireland," illustration for Reader's Digest, *May 1971. Collection of the Society of Illustrators Museum of American Illustration.*

"It's a Wise Child," illustration for Woman's Home Companion, *January 1932. The Charles Martignette Collection.*

"It's a Wise Child," illustration for Woman's Home Companion, *January 1932. The Charles Martignette Collection.*

Collection of the Society of Illustrators Museum of American Illustration.

"Old Doctor, New Doctor," illustration for Medical Times. *Collection of the Society of Illustrators Museum of American Illustration.*

Charles Marion Russell was born in Missouri to an affluent family with ancestral ties to the early West. His great uncles were fur traders and tales of their adventures stimulated the imagination of young Russell. A rebellious lad with an aversion to formal education, he left school a few days before his 16th birthday and headed for Montana Territory.

Russell became friends with trappers, traders, cowboys and Indians. He painted and sketched during long winter nights spent in trappers' cabins and cowtown saloons. Summer cowcamps and riding herd supplied him with great material for his pictures. For two years he accompanied a trapper on hunting expeditions, made hundreds of sketches and became an expert in animal anatomy.

Russell got his first job night wrangling. Wherever he went he sketched the daily events of ranch life and, from 1882 to 1892, led the life of a cowboy, drifting up and down Montana with the cattle herds. Many of his pictures were bartered to feed a friend or buy a round of drinks. But the Western frontier was beginning to change and he realized the time had come to take up the paintbrush permanently.

Russell liked working in watercolor, a medium that gave him great latitude with color, but didn't require a great deal of detail. Of all the Western painters, Russell was the most adventuresome with color. In "Scouting the Camp," opposite, he used color to draw attention to the Indians and their reflection in the water. The rest of the picture remains subdued in soft skylight.

In 1896 Russell married and settled down. His pictures began appearing on the pages of *Field and Stream, Outing* and *Sports Afield* and later, in *Scribner's, McClure's, The Saturday Evening Post* and *Leslie's Weekly*.

Financially successful, Russell began painting for his own pleasure. His paintings and bronzes commanded high prices, and are still in demand by collectors and museums. His work is in the Historical Society of Montana and a mural is in the Montana State Capitol.

"When Horseflesh Comes High," 1909. Photo courtesy of the Society of Illustrators Archives.

"Roping Fresh Mounts," 1920. Photo courtesy of the Society of Illustrators Archives.

"The Virginian," 1911. Photo courtesy of the Society of Illustrators Archives.

"Scouting the Camp." Photo courtesy of the Archives of the American Illustrators Gallery, New York City.

(1 8 5 1 - 1 9 2 8)

Arthur Burdett Frost's parents were married in 1830 in a ceremony conducted by Ralph Waldo Emerson. The Frosts were a distinguished and talented family, the most famous being the renowned poet Robert Frost, a distant cousin.

Young Frost began his career as a struggling lithographer but at the age of 23 was suddenly catapulted into fame when he illustrated the book, *Out of the Hurly Burly*, with nearly 400 pen-and-ink drawings. The book sold over a million copies, including translations into foreign languages. Two years later Frost started working with watercolors and gouache, showing great skill in that medium as well.

In 1877 he went to London for a year of study, then returned to study portraiture with Thomas Eakins at the Pennsylvania Academy of Fine Arts. He married in 1883, had two sons, and eventually settled the family in a large country estate named "Moneysunk" in Convent Station, New Jersey. Frost did his most important and memorable work during the 16 years they lived there.

Frost's career spanned nearly 50 years during which time he turned out drawings and paintings of the rural scene—farmers, barnyards, plantation life, creatures and birds of the marshes and the men who hunted them. In the hunting scene at right, even though the target is out of the picture's frame, Frost's composition gives the viewer a front row seat to the action that is about to take place. Woman and dog are perfectly poised and appear almost to have been painted on the spot.

Because he was colorblind, a member of his family had to label the colors of his palette, but despite his impaired vision he had a remarkable sense of color values.

He created the images of Tom Sawyer, Huck Finn and Uncle Remus as we now envision them, and established Br'er Rabbit as one of the classic characters in American literature.

"Grouse Hunting." Photo courtesy of Illustration House, Inc.

"In Luck," illustration for Harper's Weekly, *1884. Collection of Mr. and Mrs. Robert Crozier.*

"Ferocious Cat." Photo courtesy of the Society of Illustrators Archives.

"Black Bass Fishing," illustration for Harper's Weekly. *Collection of Mr. and Mrs. Robert Crozier.*

Magazine cover illustration, c. 1900. The Charles Martignette Collection.

ROBERT WEAVER

(1 9 2 4 - 1 9 9 4)

An imposing, highly articulate man, Robert Weaver was a socially aware being who cared deeply about the dangers to the environment and inequities in our society. He also cared about the preservation of illustration as a living representation of our culture. With a fresh and innovative approach, he used line, color and form as tools to tell us what goes on in the world around us. Shown on these pages are a few examples of the boldness with which he interpreted what he saw. As an instructor at the School of Visual Arts and as a visiting faculty member at Syracuse University, Weaver passed his concepts on to his students, urging them to go out into the world and draw real art from real life.

Weaver was born in Pittsburgh, and as a youngster devoured *The Saturday Evening Post*. The drawings of Hal Foster's Prince Valiant and Burne Hogarth's Tarzan also impressed him. He went on to study at the Carnegie Institute, then the Art Students League and the Metropolitan Museum of Art—"the best school with the best faculty." Later, when he fell in love with the heavenly light of Venice, he continued his studies at the Accademia Delle Belle Arti.

He arrived in New York with a portfolio of sketches which he took to *Town & Country* and tried to interest the magazine into hiring him as a color advisor to art directors. Instead, he was offered several manuscripts to illustrate. His knowledge of the business was so scant that when the art director spoke of "not bleeding," Weaver thought he mustn't depict violence, and "avoiding the gutter" indicated that he shouldn't show the seamier side of life.

From the late 1950s through the '70s he worked for *Esquire*, *Fortune*, *Charm* and *Seventeen*, for art directors he admired for the freedom they allowed. Art directors at *Sports Illustrated*, *Playboy*, *Life*, *Look* and Columbia Records saw the wisdom of giving Weaver full reign. The result was acclaim and awards, including a Gold Medal from the Society of Illustrators in 1964.

"College Football," illustration for Sports Illustrated. *Collection of Antonia and Francesca Weaver.*

"The Supreme Court," illustration for The New York Times Magazine. *Collection of Antonia and Francesca Weaver.*

"The Supreme Court," illustration for The New York Times Magazine. *Collection of Antonia and Francesca Weaver.*

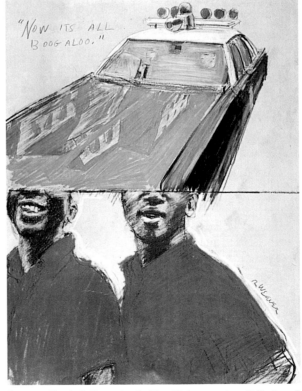

"Teenage Toughs," illustration for New York *magazine. Collection of Antonia and Francesca Weaver.*

"Charlie Parker," illustration for an album cover. Collection of Antonia and Francesca Weaver.

(1 8 8 2 - 1 9 7 1)

Illustrator, book designer, printmaker, architect, writer, lecturer, political activist—all describe Rockwell Kent, a truly remarkable man. He was, without doubt, the most important American book illustrator of his time. With strong compositions and great balance of light and dark areas he created dramatic images which reproduced beautifully in books. His work was also much in demand by advertisers such as Steinway & Sons, Rolls-Royce and American Car and Foundry Company.

Kent's father died when he was five, leaving mother and son almost penniless. His mother nevertheless saw to it that he received a good education and in 1895 Kent enrolled in the Horace Mann School in New York. He also attended the first out-of-doors summer art school in America at Shinnecock Hills, Long Island, which William Merritt Chase founded in 1891. So impressed was Chase with Kent's abilities that he offered him a full scholarship to the New York School of Art.

During the summer of 1905 Kent visited Monhegan Island off the coast of Maine and decided to stay through the winter. He worked as a teamster, longshoreman and well-driller. Though the work was exhausting he managed to paint every free moment and produced enough paintings for an exhibition in New York.

Kent's restless spirit and rigorous lifestyle played havoc with more than one of his marriages. He took extended trips to remote, rugged places unsuitable for family life. Upon his return from one such trip in 1920, Knoedler held an exhibition of his Alaskan drawings, and in 1927 Wildenstein Gallery exhibited 36 paintings he had done in Ireland.

Kent's home in the Adirondacks was struck by lightning in the 1960s and burned to the ground, destroying nearly everything, including a library of ten thousand books. The house was rebuilt, but by then Kent was in poor health and died within three months of his 89th birthday.

Illustration for Voyaging: Wayfarer, *1924. Collection of the Society of Illustrators Museum of American Illustration.*

Illustration for Voyaging: Southward From the Strait of Magellan, *1923. Courtesy of the Society of Illustrators Archives.*

"The Whale as a Dish," illustration for Moby Dick, *1930 edition. Collection of the Society of Illustrators Museum of American Illustration.*

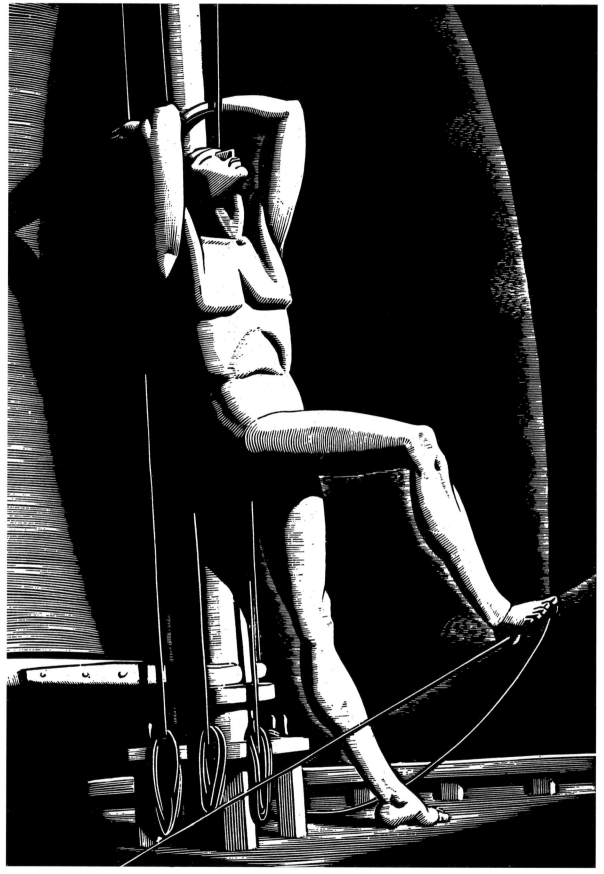

Drawing for A.C.F. Industries, 1931. Photo courtesy of Illustration House, Inc.

Unlike other caricatures—which are often of a negative, biting nature—Al Hirschfeld's do not intend to defame or exaggerate. This master of line considers himself a "characterist," rather than a caricaturist. His gift for extracting the very essence of a character's personality proves his genius lies not only in what he draws, but in what he leaves out.

Seated in his barbershop chair at his drawing board, Hirschfeld creates the fascinating drawings that have become the hallmark of his art. Sporting a handsome white beard (which he first grew in Paris because there was no hot water with which to shave) he has created a stunning number of caricatures: theater people, film stars, politicians and the literati.

Hirschfeld spent his early years in St. Louis, always drawing. When he was 11 his mother, convinced of his extraordinary talent, moved the family to New York City, which she felt would offer a more cultural climate. She rented an apartment for $4 a month in upper Manhattan, which was still farmland, and Hirschfeld began night courses at the National Academy of Art. He also attended the Art Students League, the County Council in London, and Academie Julian in Paris.

At age 17, Hirschfeld began working for the art department of Goldwyn Pictures, and a year later became the art director at Selznick International, where he stayed until 1924. While attending the theater one evening, a sketch he made on a playbill caught the eye of someone who took it to the drama editor of the *Sunday New York Herald Tribune*—and Hirschfeld's career took off. In 1925 his long relationship with *The New York Times* began.

Hirschfeld's marriage to German film star Dolly Haas lasted 52 years—until her death in 1994—and produced a daughter, Nina. Hirschfeld created the intriguing hobby of NINA-counting for *Times* readers by concealing his daughter's name in the lines of his artwork. In 1996, at age 93, the ever-youthful Hirschfeld married Louise Kerz, a theatrical historian, and continues to produce his witty, incisive images.

Diane Keaton & Woody Allen in "Annie Hall."

Spencer Tracey, Katherine Hepburn, Katherine Houghton and Sidney Poitier in "Guess Who's Coming to Dinner?"

Marlene Dietrich sings "Lili Marlene."

"Laughing Matters—America's Great Humorists."

"There's No Business Like Show Business!"

HADDON SUNDBLOM

(1 8 9 9 - 1 9 7 6)

Influenced by great painters such as John Singer Sargent, Anders Zorn and Robert Henri, Haddon Hubbard Sundblom developed a style of his own that was brilliant. The painting on the facing page is an example of his remarkable brush work, with each brush stroke carefully thought out and beautifully executed. His pictures were idealized, sunny images that made him a favorite with advertisers and public alike.

Sundblom was born in Muskegan, Michigan, the ninth child of poor Finnish parents. At 13, when his mother died, he quit school, went to work for construction firms during the day and attended art classes at night. Later, he studied at the Art Institute of Chicago and the American Academy of Art.

In 1920 he was hired by a studio as an apprentice for $10 a week. By watching McClelland Barclay and other illustrators in the studio he absorbed enough to begin getting work himself. One of his earliest assignments was to create a symbol for Quaker Oats which was used with only minor changes for over 60 years.

In 1925 he formed a studio, Stevens Sundblom & Henry, which proved to be a valuable training ground for many young artists who went on to become successful illustrators. Sundblom dominated the field of illustration in Chicago, which was then the center of the advertising world. One of the first accounts he landed for his new studio was Coca-Cola. In 1931 they asked him to create a Santa Claus to accompany the line: "The Pause that Refreshes." He continued painting Santa for the next 30 years, at first using a model, but as time went on he himself aged into the perfect Santa model.

He produced brilliant paintings for an extraordinary number of major accounts. Although he worked mostly for advertisers, he did editorial work as well and for nearly 40 years Sundblom's work was in steady demand by advertising agencies and magazines.

"Arabian Storyteller," illustration for Good Housekeeping. *Photo courtesy of Illustration House, Inc.*

"Wine—as Friendly as a Letter from Home," advertisement for the Wine Advisory Board. Photo courtesy of Illustration House, Inc.

"Santa Claus," illustration for Coca-Cola advertisement. Private collection.

Full-page advertisement in The Saturday Evening Post *for Cashmere Bouquet, May 1949. The Charles Martignette Collection.*

The tales of the Brothers Grimm, originally published in order to save folklore from being lost, must rank as the ultimate assignment for many children's book illustrators. For Maurice Sendak, these stories became a major 15-month endeavor. He traveled to Germany and Wales for background material, researched previous editions, and even purchased an original 1819 edition.

Sendak was born and grew up in Brooklyn, New York, where the excitement of street life fascinated him and provided him with material for future stories. After high school, he studied at the Art Students League, then got a job doing window display at F.A.O. Schwartz where he met an editor who gave him his first children's book assignment. Sendak was then 22 with a brilliant career ahead of him.

From 1951 to 1962 Sendak illustrated over 50 books, among them *Charlotte and the White Horse*, his first in full color, and *Kenny's Window*, the first that he also wrote. With the publication of *Where the Wild Things Are* in 1963, Sendak's career took a quantum leap. The book received the Caldecott Award but also received some chiding reviews from those who felt the images were too frightening for the young. Sendak saw it as the young hero's journey through frustration and anger to a cathartic taming of "the wild things."

His next success—and second Caldecott Award—was *In The Night Kitchen*. An illustration from that book, shown opposite, portrays the sensual pleasures of childhood—the physical sensation of kneading dough, the fun of pounding with the fists, the feelings of joy and frustration. The picture also evokes images and aromas of the kitchen and the mysteries of nocturnal New York. All this Sendak accomplishes with his deceptively simple, delightful line and flat colors.

Other facets of Sendak's career include designing for several opera and ballet productions, and an animated TV musical of "Really Rosie," which he and Carole King wrote and later adapted for the stage. In 1997 Sendak received the National Medal of Arts from President Clinton.

Detail from Where the Wild Things Are. © *1963 by Maurice Sendak.*

"Grandmother's Tale," illustration for Zlateh the Goat and Other Stories. © *1966 by Maurice Sendak.*

"He Kneaded and Punched It and Pounded and Pulled," illustration for In the Night Kitchen. *©1970 by Maurice Sendak.*

With a few deft strokes, René Bouché was able to capture the persona of the many celebrities who sat for him. His portrait of Jack Benny for CBS was almost as well known as the comedian himself, and those of Edward R. Murrow and Ed Sullivan became media trademarks. Among others whose portraits he painted were W.H. Auden, Igor Stravinsky, Elsa Maxwell, Sophia Loren and William and Elaine DeKooning. He dominated the fashion and portraiture field for two decades prior to his death.

Bouché painted loosely in oil with thin paint applications and empty areas of bare canvas. His portraits were keenly observed, penetrating likenesses, exquisitely drawn and freely painted with an air of spontaneity and informality. His seemingly effortless approach is apparent in the charming portrait at right. With a minimum of lines he captured the elegant bearing of the woman, and with a few flicks of the brush, the adorable dog in her arms.

Born in Prague, Chechoslovakia, Bouché began working as an advertising illustrator in Berlin at the age of 22. In 1933, he left for Paris where he received his only significant, formal art training. His early fashion drawings appeared in Paris *Vogue* in 1938. It was the beginning of a long and fruitful association with *Vogue*, both in New York and in Paris, that lasted throughout his lifetime.

There followed a very productive and financially rewarding period when, in addition to his editorial work, he began working for advertising clients such as Saks Fifth Avenue, Schweppes, Jaguar and Helena Rubinstein. His free, loose, watercolor paintings for Elizabeth Arden established an identity and distinction known as "The Arden Look."

In 1948 he became involved with the abstract expressionism school of painting and joined the Eighth Street Avant-Garde Painters Club. Within six years, however, he had lost interest and thereafter devoted himself to portraiture.

Illustration for Elizabeth Arden Ideal Suntan Oil advertisement in Vogue *magazine, July 1944.*

Fashion illustration. Collection of the Society of Illustrators Museum of American Illustration.

"At the Villa," 1957. Collection of the Society of Illustrators Museum of American Illustration.

Fashion illustration. Collection of the Society of Illustrators Museum of American Illustration.

"Sunday Stroll." Collection of Arpi Ermoyan.

PRUETT CARTER

A sense of dignity and good taste are the hallmarks of Pruett A. Carter's illustrations. His heroines, noted for their gentle, patrician beauty, were portrayed against equally refined backgrounds. As though directing a film or a play, Carter always took great pains in planning the source of light and the design of both set and costumes. The painting on the facing page is a good example of how his superb composition and theatrical lighting draw the viewer's attention to the young woman's hand. The warm light from the lamp adds a soft, mellow glow to the scene.

Born in Missouri, Carter was raised on an Indian reservation in Wyoming where his father ran a trading post and his mother taught school. When Carter was in his teens the family moved to California where he attended the Los Angeles Art School.

At 19 he moved to New York and landed a job drawing borders for Hearst's *Journal American*. Transferred to the *Atlanta Journal* he did reportorial drawings until Hearst moved him back to New York, promoting him to art editor of *Good Housekeeping* magazine.

Carter's career was interrupted by World War I. After serving as a lieutenant in the Army Carter returned to *Good Housekeeping* briefly, then struck out on his own as a free-lance illustrator.

Harry Quinan, the famous art editor at *Woman's Home Companion*, gave him his first professional assignment for an opening spread in the 1918 Easter issue. For over 40 years thereafter his illustrations appeared regularly in *The Ladies' Home Journal*, *The Delineator*, *McCall's*, *Pictorial Review*, *Good Housekeeping*, *American*, *Collier's* and other national magazines.

Carter pursued a dual career—in addition to illustrating, he was a fine teacher. For many years he taught at the Grand Central Art School in New York City. After moving to California in 1930 he became affiliated with the Chouinard Art Institute in Los Angeles and served as head of its illustration department for over 25 years.

"Troubador," illustration for American *magazine. Collection of the Society of Illustrators Museum of American Illustration.*

"Manhattan Jungle," illustration for American *magazine, March 1941. Photo courtesy of Illustration House, Inc.*

Advertisement for Elgin Watch, 1926. Photo courtesy of Illustration House, Inc.

"Ballerina," illustration for McCall's *magazine, October 1929. Collection of the Society of Illustrators Museum of American Illustration.*

Science writer Isaac Asimov once called Robert Theodore McCall "the nearest thing to an artist-in-residence from outer space."

McCall is renowned throughout the world for his soaring murals and canvasses, and for his postage stamps commemorating the space accomplishments of the United States. His "Decade of Achievement" stamp was cancelled on the Moon before a world-wide television audience. McCall's painting on the opposite page, of Neil Armstrong and Edwin "Buzz" Aldrin—the first two men on the moon—vividly captures the drama of that epic event. Worthy of special note, aside from the true

artistry in all of McCall's pictures, are his magnificent skies and clouds.

Born in Columbus, Ohio, to parents who encouraged his interest in art, he won a scholarship to Columbus School of Fine Art and by age 17 was working as a part-time commercial artist. During World War II he served with the Army Air Corps, sketching airplanes whenever possible.

In 1949 McCall moved to New York where he began illustrating for the major magazines and advertising agencies. Among his many commissions for *Life* magazine was a series of paintings of the future of space flight. When the National Aeronautics & Space Administration in Washington, D.C., initiated its Fine Art Program, McCall was assigned to cover the Mercury, Gemini and Apollo missions.

Because of his vision and lifelong interest in the subject, McCall has been able to accurately depict future exploration of space years in advance of actual events. He created conceptual paintings for "2001: A Space Odyssey," and spectacular art for films such as "Star Trek," "Meteor" and "The Black Hole." His 6-story high mural, "The Space Mural a Cosmic View," celebrates our first manned lunar adventure, and is visited each year by over 10 million visitors to the National Air and Space Museum. At Walt Disney's EPCOT Center in Florida he created a 19- by 60-foot canvas, "The Prologue and the Promise." Other murals are on permanent display at the Johnson Space Center in Texas and the Dryden Flight Research Facility in California.

"Opening the Space Frontier—The Next Giant Step," 1979. Detail of the 16' x 72' mural depicting the first two decades of American space exploration. Collection of NASA/Johnson Space Center.

"Starsailor," 1996. Conceptual study for a proposed new science fiction film. Collection of the artist.

"Threshold," 1983. Collection of NASA.

"First Men on the Moon," 1971. On July 20, 1969, Neil Armstrong and Edwin E. Aldrin became the first humans to set foot on an alien world, the Earth's moon. It was the culmination of the largest scientific and technological undertaking in human history. Collection of Broadway National Bank, San Antonio, Texas.

"Rocketplane 2050," 1996. Created for the Centennial issue of The New York Times Magazine. *Collection of the artist.*

"The Spirit of Iridium," 1996. Designed to dramatize Motorola's new satellite system for global voice communication. Collection of Motorola, Inc., © 1996 Motorola, Inc. All right reserved.

"The Spirit of Challenger," 1995. Commemorates the loss of the space shuttle Challenger on January 28, 1986. Collection of The Challenger for Space Education.

E R T É

(1 8 9 2 - 1 9 9 0)

For over seven decades Erté's designs for women's fashions and his set decorations for both stage and screen had a considerable influence upon the culture and style of the 20th century. His intense and meticulously executed illustrative work combines the rhythmical sensuality of a Beardsley with the breathless elegance of a Persian miniature. His colorful visions, rendered in gouache and accented with metallic paints, bristle with fanciful charm and evoke in the viewer a passion for far-off times and exotic places.

Born Romain de Tirtoff in St. Petersburg, he was the privileged son of Russian aristocrats in the affluent era before the Revolution. His parents exposed him to opera and ballet at an early age, thus cultivating in him an appreciation for music and the theater. He enrolled at the Academie Julian in Paris where he studied briefly with the French painter Jean-Paul Laurens. In 1913 he began designing dresses for Paul Pioret, a leading producer of women's fashions. The pseudonym Erté evolved from the earlier use of his initials, R.T., and first appeared in print during his tenure with Pioret.

Erté moved to Monte Carlo in 1914 and became a contributor to *Harper's Bazar* (later spelled Bazaar). His work caught the attention of William Randolph Hearst, who hired him for his motion picture company, Cosmopolitan Films. Hearst's friend, Louis B. Mayer, invited Erté to Hollywood in 1925 and signed him to an exclusive contract, but after waiting 18 months for Mayer's projects to materialize, Erté became frustrated and left.

Luminaries such as Florenz Ziegfield, George White, Earl Carroll and the Schuberts kept Erté busy producing a great number of set and costume designs until the 1929 Depression cut Broadway production budgets.

In 1967 the Grosvenor Galleries in London and New York hosted exhibitions of Erté's art, reminding the world of the elegance and style of a period gone by.

"Au Reveil du Passe," 1923. A.J. Fine Arts Ltd. & Sevenarts, Ltd. © Sevenarts, Ltd.

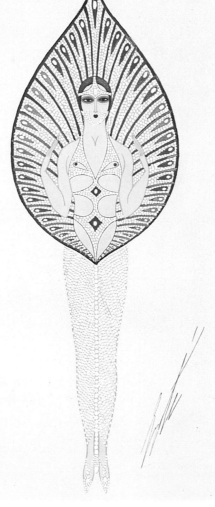

"Le Diamant Les Pierres," 1929. A.J. Fine Arts Ltd. & Sevenarts, Ltd. © Sevenarts, Ltd.

"Le Harem Moderne," 1918. A.J. Fine Arts Ltd. & Sevenarts, Ltd. © Sevenarts, Ltd.

"Design for Madame Walska La Contessa Nocis DeFigaro," 1923. A.J. Fine Arts Ltd. & Sevenarts, Ltd. © Sevenarts, Ltd.

"L'Oiseaux Merveillieux," 1927. A.J. Fine Arts Ltd. & Sevenarts, Ltd. © Sevenarts, Ltd.

J O H N   H E L D   J R .

(1 8 8 9 - 1 9 5 8)

No one depicted the liberated generation of the 1920s better than John Held, Jr. Irreverent black-and-white drawings showing flappers in short skirts and bobbed hair dancing the Charleston and drinking bathtub gin appeared in *College Humor*, *Judge*, *Life*, *Cosmopolitan*, *Vanity Fair* and *The New Yorker*. Advertisers such as Van Heusen, Packard and Tintex also besieged him with work. One frustrated advertiser, turned down because of Held's overloaded schedule, gave him a blank check and told him to fill in his own price.

The travel poster for the New Haven Railroad on the facing page is characteristic of the style that made him famous. Drawn with a minimum of detail, the silhouetted shapes of the animated figures tell the story at a glance.

Held was born a Mormon in Salt Lake City. While still in his teens he learned to make engravings for his father's stationery business and decided to become an artist. After he married, he sent his pretty young wife out to solicit work. She succeeded, sold work as her own and signed it "Myrtle." Only after the couple split up did Held reveal his identity. With residences in New York and Florida, and a farm in Connecticut, he entertained lavishly and went through two more wives.

The 1929 stock market crash had a sobering effect on the country and Held found himself out of step with the grim realities of the Depression. Publishers stopped buying his brand of humor. To make matters worse, he lost most of his money to the fraudulent scheme of Ivar Kreugar, the Swedish match king. Held turned to sculpting in ceramics and set up a forge, making handsome weather vanes, signs and andirons out of wrought iron. He spent the remaining years of his life with his fourth wife, running a small farm in Belmar, New Jersey.

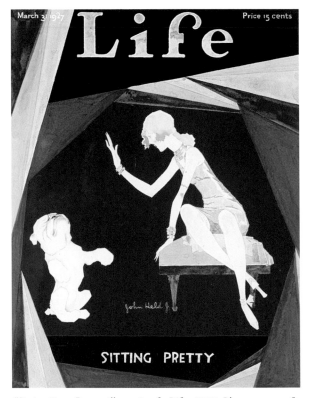

"Sitting Pretty," cover illustration for Life, *1927. Photo courtesy of Illustration House, Inc.*

"James claims that Smith's necktie is to blame for his slicing." Photo courtesy of Illustration House, Inc.

"Hog Island." Collection of the Society of Illustrators Museum of American Illustration.

"Flaming Youth." Collection of the Society of Illustrators Museum of American Illustration.

"Grandma in the Garden," illustration for Judge *magazine, May 5, 1923. Photo courtesy of the Society of Illustrators Archives.*

"Northward," poster for the New Haven Railroad. Photo courtesy of Illustration House, Inc.

ARTHUR KELLER

(1 8 6 6 - 1 9 2 4)

From the turn of the century until his death, Arthur Igantius Keller's illustrations graced the pages of the leading periodicals of the day. His preliminary studies show a mastery of drawing, the result of his lengthy and thorough training. He became an accomplished artist whose work was compared to the French master Watteau.

Born in New York of German immigrant parents, Keller at 17 entered the National Academy of Design, and at the age of 24 went to Munich and spent a year studying under the German classical painter Ludwig von Loefftz. Upon his return to America he was hired by the *New York Herald* as an illustrator. Following this stint at the newspaper he began illustrating for magazines such as *The Delineator*, *Cosmopolitan*, *McClure's*, *Scribner's*, *Harper's*, *The Ladies' Home Journal*, *Century* and the *Sunday Magazine*. Within a short time he was working for book publishers as well.

Keller's book illustration on the facing page is a fine example of his painting style. While the look is spontaneous in nature, and appears to have been painted from life, he has nevertheless taken care to include all necessary details. By using a full value range on the woman's head, and adding a bit more detail to that area, Keller forces the eye to the central figure.

The Kellers lived in Riverdale, New York, and summered in Cragsmoor, a colony of accomplished artists in the Shawangunk Mountains. His homes were filled with antiques, costumes and reference books, all used to help him create authentic settings for each illustration. He made graphic notes about his research, compiled them into two volumes which were published in 1920 under the title, "Figure Studies from Life." He won numerous awards in America and abroad.

Keller was a charter member of the Society of Illustrators and served as its president in 1903. In 1925 the Society held a memorial exhibition in his honor and in January of 1989 displayed a retrospective exhibition of his work.

"The Prince of Graustark." Collection of the Society of Illustrators Museum of American Illustration.

"Hidden Children." Collection of the Society of Illustrators Museum of American Illustration.

"The Fortunate Youth," illustration for The Delineator *magazine, 1913. Collection of the Society of Illustrators Museum of American Illustration.*

"Marrakesh." Collection of the Society of Illustrators Museum of American Illustration.

Illustration for a story published by Houghton, Mifflin & Company, 1905. Photo courtesy of Illustration House, Inc.

BURT SILVERMAN

(b . 1 9 2 8)

Amaster draftsman and superb painter, Burton Silverman creates each picture with great sensitivity and intensity. The painterly quality of his work and his keen observation of people have resulted in brilliant portraits of world leaders and noted personalities. He appears to capture the very essence of his subjects quickly with skillful, loose brushwork. In the illustration for *American Heritage* on the facing page we see how astutely he has captured the character and mood of the two men strolling down the avenue.

At the age of nine he attended Saturday art classes at Pratt Institute in his native Brooklyn and later went to the High School of Music and Art in New York City. He made the Metropolitan Museum of Art his second home, learning from the Masters: Jan van Eyck, Velázquez, Rembrandt, Degas, Eakins, Homer and Sargent. Following his graduation from Columbia University in 1949 and studio courses at the Art Students League, Silverman began his dual career as illustrator and easel painter. His illustrations have appeared in such major magazines as *Time*, *Newsweek*, *New York*, *Esquire* and *Sports Illustrated*. His elegant portraits opened the "Profile" section of *The New Yorker* for 25 years.

Silverman has often been called upon to do an illustration or a series of pictures of an event where no visible record exists, such as the shooting down of the Korean 747 airliner, for which *Time* gave him a five-hour deadline. Another assignment required 90 drawings of the Founding Fathers in realistic situations showing emotional responses. The resulting work breathed life into the men who had previously been seen only in stiff, formal poses and settings.

In addition to the dozens of awards he has won from annual exhibitions such as those of the National Academy of Design and the American Watercolor Society, Silverman has also had numerous one-man shows in New York, Philadelphia, Houston, Boston and Washington, D.C.

"Echoes That Remain," illustration for a film by Weisenthal Center, 1991. Collection of the artist.

"John and Yoko: A Love Story," movie poster for NBC, 1985. Collection of the artist.

"Deng Zhao Ping Comes Visiting," cover illustration for Time *magazine. © 1979 Time Inc. Collection of the National Portrait Gallery. Photo courtesy of the artist.*

"A Time to Build," illustration for UJA-Federation Capital Campaign. Private collection.

"A Short and Scary Walk with Andrew Jackson," illustration for American Heritage, October 1992. *Photo courtesy of the artist.*

For all his success and stature as one of the most honored illustrators of his era, Robert Riggs was remarkably free of imitators. He created powerful pictures with monumental concepts that defied imitation. It is apparent from the complicated composition of Washington landing in New York, opposite, that Riggs felt the art had to be quite large in scope in order to tell the whole story within one painting.

Born in Decatur, Illinois, Riggs studied for two years at James Milliken University and a year at the Art Students League. He served in the Army during World War I and remained in Paris after the war to study at the Academie Julian. Upon returning to the United States he took a job in Philadelphia as a sketch artist for the N.W. Ayer advertising agency.

He settled the question of whether to pursue commercial or fine art by doing both. After a frustrating attempt at abstract painting he turned to lithography, where he could develop his pictures on stone and control every stage of the process. His favorite subjects were the circus and prize fights. For the galleries he worked in the traditional manner and for illustration he used scratchboard and litho crayon. His gallery work caught the attention of publishers and advertisers alike and brought him many assignments from both sources. He also began painting again, but this time, realistically.

An avid traveler to exotic places, Riggs lived in a museum of his own creation. Rooms were thickly covered from floor to ceiling with his collection of ceremonial masks, tomahawks, African relics, primitive drums, skulls, snakes and all manner of oddities brought back from all parts of the world.

Riggs fought a losing battle with diabetes but continued to work and completed some of his finest work just before his death. His prints are in major museums, including the Library of Congress, the Brooklyn Museum, Philadelphia Museum of Fine Arts and the Metropolitan Museum of Art in New York.

"The Boxers," study for Johnny Walker Black Label Scotch advertisement. Collection of the Society of Illustrators Museum of American Illustration.

Advertisement for John Hancock Mutual Life Insurance Company.

"Washington Arriving in New York for his Inauguration." Photo courtesy of Illustration House, Inc.

During his brief lifetime, Morton Roberts completed an astonishing number of paintings for publication in magazines as well as for exhibition in galleries throughout the Northeast.

Born in Worcester, Massachusetts, Roberts was a child prodigy whose father struggled to provide him with all the costly art materials needed to satisfy the boy's talent. The precocious youngster produced many paintings and watercolors of New England life. He went on to study at the Yale School of Fine Arts and graduated with honors, having completed the five-year course in three years.

Roberts illustrated scores of assignments for prominent magazines such as *McCall's*, *Redbook*, *Reader's Digest* and *Sports Illustrated*. For *Life* magazine he painted a fifteen-page series depicting Verdi's opera "Rigoletto," another series on the origins of jazz, and some outstanding pictures of Rasputin in an article on Russian history.

In the illustration on the facing page Roberts' composition is so well conceived that although the main character of the story, Lenin, is off to the left side of the picture, the eye is immediately drawn to him by the strategically placed red flag. The horizontal line formed by the tops of the soldiers' heads also leads the eye directly to him.

Having achieved success in both illustration and gallery painting, murals seemed the next logical step in his development as an artist. He began working on canvases of ever-increasing size, while his imagery became correspondingly bolder and the scale of the figures more heroic. Roberts' last commission was the execution of a vast series of murals commemorating the life and achievements of General Douglas MacArthur. He worked long and hard on the ebony pencil cartoons which hinted at the great work that was to come. Tragically, however, at the age of 37 he suddenly died of a heart attack.

Many of Roberts' works have found their way into private collections as well as prominent institutions such as Yale University, Carnegie Institute, National Academy of Design and European museums.

"Rigoletto," illustration for Life *magazine. Collection of Jean Hunnicutt.*

"Christmas Carolers," illustration for Collier's *magazine. Private collection.*

"Rigoletto," illustration for Life *magazine. Collection of Jean Hunnicutt.*

"The Grand Marshall." Collection of Jean Hunnicutt.

"Lenin Addressing Troops," illustration for Life *magazine, 1959. Photo courtesy of Illustration House, Inc.*

At the height of the rivalry between *The Saturday Evening Post* and *Collier's* magazines, Donald Teague, who worked for both, found it prudent to use a pseudonym for his work in *Collier's*, as in the signature on the facing page. His thorough craftsmanship, strong composition and painting skills, however, did not change.

Living near the movie industry in California gave Teague easy access to the Western subjects for which his paintings are noted. Cowboys who worked as actors and stunt men in the

1930s and early '40s were more than happy to pose for him, and relics of pioneer streets and buildings on the movie lots served as settings for many of his illustrations. The Pacific Ocean also offered Teague background material for his illustrations of the sea, another of his favorite subjects.

Teague was born in Brooklyn and studied at the Art Students League under Bridgman and DuMond. After a stint in the Navy, he returned to New York in 1918 and got a job illustrating two stories for *The Delineator* magazine. There followed an assignment from *The Saturday Evening Post* and from that point on his career was launched.

Until 1923 Teague had been working in oils, but a water-

color sketching trip abroad was a turning point in his career. Watercolor became his medium from then on—one he never tired of because it possessed a quality he called "verve." He spent three or four months each year traveling, always sketching.

For many years Teague lived in New Rochelle, New York, but in 1938, after he married, the couple moved to Los Angeles. At the height of his 38-year illustration career, one of Teague's leading clients, *Collier's*, stopped publication. Teague took this as an omen and turned his energies to painting landscapes. His work has been in the Metropolitan Museum of Art, the National Academy of Design, the Royal Watercolor Society in London and many other collections.

"Waiting for Trouble."

"Street Scene, Sorrento."

Illustration for The Saturday Evening Post. *The Charles Martignette Collection.*

"*My Father's Child,*" *illustration for* Collier's *magazine, 1953.*

The subject of children and their mothers was never more beautifully idealized than by Jessie Willcox Smith. Her identification with children is unparalleled in illustration, a gift she discovered only fortuitously when she was 17. She had been teaching kindergarten when she was invited to act as chaperone while her cousin gave art instruction to a young male professor. Smith discovered the joy of drawing, stopped teaching and enrolled at Mrs. Sarah Peter's School of Design for Women in Philadelphia, the city where she had been born.

She then studied briefly at the Pennsylvania Academy of the Arts under Thomas Eakins, found the atmosphere too dour and left to begin illustrating professionally in 1888. Her first published piece appeared in the May 1888 issue of *St. Nicholas Magazine*.

The person who most influenced her work was Howard Pyle. As one of his first students at Drexel Institute in Philadelphia, she found that the force of his spirit and overall view of illustration shaped the way she created pictures thereafter.

From the large painting reproduced on the opposite page, Smith's full range and versatility can be seen in her imaginative portrayal of the leading characters in "Alice in Wonderland." Her keen eye, along with her innate feelings about children, enabled her to portray them in a stylized and most favorable light. Many of her finished illustrations retained her exquisite line drawings, over which she applied color.

Smith developed a lifelong friendship with two other Pyle students, Violet Oakley and Elizabeth Shippen Green, which led to a long period when the three shared studio and living space.

Smith's work, executed in mixed media, appeared in most of the popular magazines including *Century*, *Collier's*, *Good Housekeeping*, *Scribner's* and *Woman's Home Companion*. As one of the country's most successful illustrators, Smith augmented her substantial income with private portrait commissions. Her many books became classics, all of which were for or about children, and even as an adult she herself retained the frank sweetness of a child.

"Noah's Ark," illustration for The Bed-Time Book, *published by Chatto & Windus, 1907. Photo courtesy of Illustration House, Inc.*

"I Know That Man," advertisement for Cream of Wheat, 1909. Collection of the Society of Illustrators Museum of American Illustration. On loan from NABISCO, Inc.

"How Doth the Busy Bee," illustration for A Child's Book of Old Verses. © 1910 Duffield & Co. Collection of Kendra Krienke and Allan Daniel.*

"Alice in Wonderland," book cover of Boys and Girls of Bookland. *© 1923 David McKay & Co. Collection of Kendra Krienke and Allan Daniel.*

Carl Sandburg, who had posed for a portrait by William Arthur Smith, paid him the following tribute: "When he paints bug, leaf, animal, antique head, old worn house or fresh child face, his prayer is to be inside of it as part of what gives it personal identity and inviolable dignity."

Whether painting the tough, sinewy boxers below, or the fashionable model, right, Smith never failed to capture the mood and setting of the scene. His range of painting skills was vast—from the fresh, loose style as in Einstein's portrait below, to the more commercially-oriented illustrations used in advertising, to the painterly quality he achieved in his gallery work.

Born in Toledo, Ohio, Smith studied at the University of Toledo and Keane's Art School. He arrived in New York at the age of 19, began illustrating for the pulps and comic strips, and continued studying at Grand Central Art School and the Art Students League. He later attended l'Ecole des Beaux-Arts and l'Academie de la Grand Chaumiere in Paris.

In 1942 he received his first magazine illustration commission from *Cosmopolitan*. Over the years Smith received assignments from many other magazines as well, including *The Saturday Evening Post*, *Redbook*, *True*, *This Week*, *Life* and *Reader's Digest*.

Smith's art was distinguished by its painterly quality and excellent draftsmanship. His long career was divided between teaching, painting for exhibition, and illustrating for books, magazines and advertising clients. Along the way, he also painted murals and explored printmaking. He was expertly equipped for assignments with international backgrounds as a result of his World War II experience with the Office of Strategic Services in China where he worked on psychological warfare projects.

In addition to the many honors he received here, Smith lectured and had one-man exhibitions in more than 20 cities of Europe and Asia. His paintings are in the Metropolitan Museum of Art, the Los Angeles Museum and many other collections.

"During Intermission...The Pause that Refreshes," illustration for Coca-Cola advertisement, c. 1960. The Charles Martignette Collection.

"He is Everybody's Trusted Friend," illustration of Einstein for John Hancock Life Insurance Co., 1960.

"Ten Minutes to Live," illustration for The Saturday Evening Post, *c. 1950. The Charles Martignette Collection.*

"Boxing Scene," illustration for The Saturday Evening Post. *Collection of the James A. Michener Art Museum.*

Illustration for Good Housekeeping *magazine. Photo courtesy of the Society of Illustrators Archives.*

Reigning among the top illustrators from the 1950s through the 1970s, Joe Bowler enriched the national magazines with his beautifully rendered, romantic paintings.

Born in Forest Hills, New York, Bowler began drawing at the age of three and knew by the time he reached high school that illustration was to become his career. Following graduation, Bowler took a job in an art studio, earning $18 a week. In 1947 he joined the Charles E. Cooper Studios where he flourished among a group of the most distinguished illustrators of the day. At the same time he took evening classes at the Art Students League, studying under Frank Reilly, Robert Hale and Howard Trafton.

Bowler attributes his first break into the "big time" to Coby Whitmore, a "star" at Cooper's who, while delivering his own assignment to *Cosmopolitan* magazine, took along a sample of Bowler's which the art director bought on the spot. Within six months Bowler had illustrations in five leading magazines. Because of his sensitive portrayal of people, Bowler was called upon by the magazines to do portraits of celebrities such as the Kennedys, Eisenhowers and Charles deGaulle.

In 1958 Bowler contracted polio but undaunted, he painted while in a wheelchair and within three months had an illustration published in *The Saturday Evening Post*. His seven-year period of recovery turned out to be a turning point in his career. He began seriously studying the Old Masters and made a transition from illustration to portraiture.

Bowler's very tender painting of the charming young lady on the facing page exemplifies his great skill at portraiture. His controlled use of color and soft lighing accentuates the gentle, cuddly quality of the subject. Laying washes of transparent glaze over carefully done pencil drawings on gessoed surfaces, Bowler's painterly skills create a breathing likeness.

The Artists Guild of New York named Bowler "Artist of the Year" in 1967, and the Society of Illustrators elected him to its Hall of Fame in 1992.

"The Baker Rubies," illustration for Collier's. *The Charles Martignette Collection.*

"A Love Story," illustration for Cosmopolitan *magazine, May 1967. Collection of Arpi Ermoyan.*

"First Love, The Second Time." Collection of the Society of Illustrators Museum of American Illustration.

"The Eyelet Dress." Collection of the Society of Illustrators Museum of American Illustration.

Edwin A. Georgi was an engineering student and handsome football star at Princeton when World War I broke out. He volunteered and served as a pilot in the U.S. Air Force, and when the war was over he got a job doing paste-ups in the art department of an advertising agency.

Under the guidance of noted artist and art director René Clarke, Georgi learned his craft well and soon became known for his powerful illustrations for the Hartford Fire Insurance Company. At the same time, his work for Crane paper advertisements pictured elegant women in social settings. He had several other prominent clients, among them Stetson Hats, Hokanum Woolens, Yardley Soap, Studebaker and U.S. Steel.

Georgi's ability to depict beautiful women also caught the attention of the national magazines. His exciting explorations in color happily coincided with the introduction of color gravure by the Crowell-Collier publishing group in the late 1930s. The increased use of color in their magazines, together with Georgi's unique new style, rejuvenated his career and his work began appearing regularly in their publications. In addition to his work for *Woman's Home Companion*, *American* and *Collier's*, his illustrations appeared in many other magazines, including *Cosmopolitan*, *McCall's* and *Redbook*.

Georgi's illustrations took on a startling new look when, after many years of working with muted, subtle tones, he suddenly discovered vivid color. Using a pointillist approach, he began breaking up his color into small strokes, juxtaposing a spectrum of warm and cool colors and values throughout the picture. Although his work remained realistic, he kept pushing the limits of reality with this unusual treatment of color. The effect was vibrant and exciting, giving his pictures great impact on the printed page.

A painstaking perfectionist, Georgi sometimes did his pictures over two or three times to achieve the most dramatic effect. He was also an enthusiastic musician and composer of popular songs which were recorded by Columbia Records.

Photo courtesy of Illustration House, Inc.

"The Key," illustration for Woman's Home Companion, *January 1947. Collection of the Society of Illustrators Museum of American Illustration.*

"Call You Up Sometime," illustration for Redbook *magazine, September 1956. The Charles Martignette Collection.*

"The Secret." Photo courtesy of Illustration House, Inc.

(1 9 0 2 - 1 9 7 0)

During the 1930s Lord & Taylor's art director, Harry Rodman, designed a format for the store's advertising which became known as "The Lord & Taylor Look." Dorothy Hood's beautifully drawn fashion illustrations were an important part of that "look." Her black-and-white wash technique was ideal for newspaper reproduction, and her unique style immediately identified the ad as one of Lord & Taylor's. All her work was done to size, insuring that reproduction would be as faithful as possible to the original art.

Working directly from life, Hood posed her models in attitudes depicting real-life activities that women could identify with. By introducing little touches to the backgrounds—a chandelier here, a spray of flowers there—she gave a bit more dimension to the scene. Her work reflected the high-quality status of the department store and gave the public a sense of how the well-dressed American woman should look. So successful was her art in selling merchandise that her work for Lord & Taylor continued to appear in newspapers and magazines for decades.

Hood was born in New Holland, Pennsylvania, and attended the New York School of Applied Design. She met Rodman while both were working at Macy's. Recognizing the extraordinary talent of the young artist, he whisked her away to Lord & Taylor when he became art director there. Because her studio was located near the department store, models and merchandise—as well as her artwork—could quickly and easily travel back and forth. Short deadlines faced by fashion illustrators presented no problem for her.

While touring Bermuda on a motor bike one day in the 1950s, she had an accident that seriously injured her right arm. Undeterred by this disability, she taught herself to draw with her left hand and was so successful that only her intimate friends were aware of the difficult transition she had undergone.

Dorothy Hood continued illustrating for Lord & Taylor until her death on March 17, 1970.

Fashion Institute of Technology, Frances Neady collection.

Fashion Institute of Technology, Frances Neady collection.

Fashion Institute of Technology, Frances Neady collection.

Fashion Institute of Technology, Frances Neady collection.

Fashion Institute of Technology, Frances Neady collection.

Collection of the Society of Illustrators Museum of American Illustration.

ROBERT McGINNIS

(b . 1 9 2 6)

One of the busiest and most prolific painters of paperback cover art, Robert McGinnis has worked for virtually all the publishers in that field, as well as for many magazines such as *The Saturday Evening Post, Good Housekeeping, Reader's Digest, The Ladies' Home Journal, True* and *McCall's*. McGinnis was born in Cincinnati, Ohio. His father, who liked to draw cartoons, taught the youngster how to draw "Popeye," and McGinnis did become a cartoonist

for a short time. His high school teacher wrote a letter of recommendation to the Disney studios, who hired him as an art apprentice. World War II intervened, however; the studio was disbanded, and McGinnis joined the Merchant Marines. After he returned from sea duty, he studied at Ohio State University and the Central Academy of Commercial Art in Cincinnati, then worked for a time at Chaite Studio where he turned out many illustrations for advertisers.

In addition to his editorial and advertising work, McGinnis has illustrated many movie posters, including four James Bond films, Jane Fonda's "Barbarella," Burt Reynolds' "Gator," and the titles for "Hallelujah Trail." His painting for "The Searchers"

on the facing page visually evokes the sadness of the whole story in one frame. John Wayne, with shoulders slumped, leans forward to better see the doll left by his niece, while his sister-in-law's shawl hangs limply from his hand. This painting won a Silver Medal from the Society of Illustrators and has been willed by the purchaser to the John Wayne Cancer Center at U.C.L.A. in California.

In the early 1980s McGinnis began painting Westerns in addition to his commercial work, and became very involved in fine art gallery painting. His work is highly sought after and is held in many private collections around the country.

"Love Child," illustration for Reader's Digest Condensed Books, *1992. Collection of the Society of Illustrators Museum of American Illustration.*

"Renee Streim." Collection of Mr. and Mrs. Gerald McConnell.

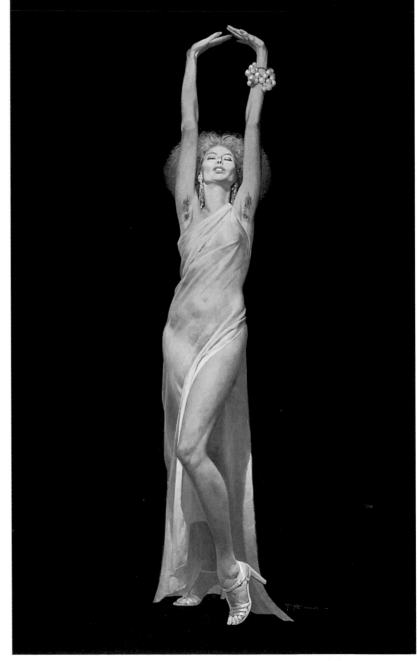

"Mariska," illustration for Berkley Books, 1981. Collection of the Society of Illustrators Museum of American Illustration.

"Ethan," illustration for the film "The Searchers." Private collection.

"Capitol Reef." Collection of Mrs. Emily Filley.

"Father of the Bride," illustration for Good Housekeeping. *Collection of the artist.*

"Slava." Collection of Donald R. Johnson.

"Wreck of the Cencepcion," illustration for the National Geographic Society.

The cartoons and caricatures of Thomas Nast had an enormous impact on American politics of the mid- to late-19th century. With piercing observations he unveiled to the public the human folly, greed and hypocrisy of the political system. He believed in social justice, politicians' accountability to their constituencies, and equitable treatment of all people, regardless of race.

Nast was born in Germany and moved to New York with his family when he was five. With little formal art training, at age 15 he began illustrating for *Frank Leslie's Illustrated News*.

Later he traveled to England, Sicily and Calabria, following Garibaldi's Army. Upon his return to America in 1861 he produced many war-related illustrations for *Harper's Weekly*. President Lincoln considered Nast one of the most influential recruiters for the Northern cause.

Following the Civil War, during the reign of the Tammany political machine in New York, Nast developed his most effective style in attacking the corrupt Boss Tweed. In one cartoon Tweed's features were completely eliminated, replaced by a money bag stamped with a dollar sign, sitting atop his bulging figure. Tweed was eventually jailed and driven out of office due in large part to Nast's relentless campaign against his manipulation of New York's political machine.

The gentle, sentimental side of Nast was revealed every Christmas season in *Harper's*. Drawing from European traditions, he created the American version of Santa Claus shown on the facing page—a bearded, jovial fellow whom he depicted with great assurance and love. Haddon Sundblom and others later refined the jolly old character into Santa as we know him today. Nast also created the Republican 'elephant' and the Democratic 'donkey,' and was an accomplished painter of historical scenes.

At the time of his death in Ecuador, where he was serving as the American consul-general, he had experienced two decades of declining appreciation for his work. But the fact that today his illustrations are so highly regarded is testament to his great vision and talent.

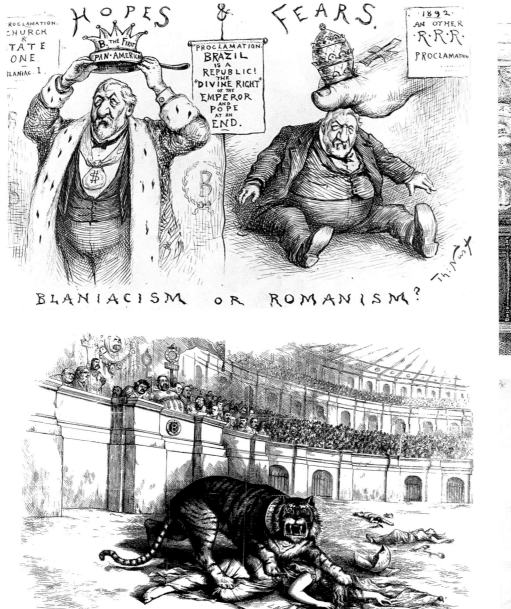

"Blaniacism or Romanism?" Collection of the Society of Illustrators Museum of American Illustration.

Photo courtesy of the Society of Illustrators Archives.

Photo courtesy of the Society of Illustrators Archives.

"Only a Matter of Time." Photo courtesy of the Society of Illustrators Archives.

"Santa Claus." Photo courtesy of the Society of Illustrators Archives.

What came to be known as the "Fade-away Girl" was the unique manner in which Coles Phillips designed many of his pictures. By careful preliminary planning of shapes, he tied the figures in his pictures into the background by either color, value or pattern, leaving it to the viewer's imagination to connect all the missing parts. An example of that unusual technique appears in a few of the illustrations below. His painting for Holeproof Hosiery, opposite, is evidence of his great sense of design and reflects his exquisite taste in portraying delicate, beautiful women.

Born in Springfield, Ohio, Phillips attended Kenyon College where his first published work appeared in the college newspaper and yearbook. Impatient to pursue his career, he left college after his Junior year and headed for New York. After a series of part-time jobs and night classes at the Chase School of Art, he went to work for an advertising agency as a sketch artist and learned the inner workings well enough to start his own agency in 1906. He missed the artistic side of the business, however, and closed the agency to become a free-lance illustrator.

When editors of the old *Life*, then a humorous weekly, asked Phillips to come up with a fresh approach for their covers, he decided to use the "Fade-away Girl" device. It was a great success and for two decades thereafter, the "Fade-away Girl" became a regular feature of Phillips' covers for *Life*, *Collier's*, *Liberty*, *The Saturday Evening Post*, *Good Housekeeping* and *Vogue*. His illustrations of beautiful women were sought by advertisers as well.

By 1924 Phillips had developed a serious kidney problem and went abroad for a year to seek help from European specialists. None could help him so he returned home, unable to continue working, and died at the age of 47.

"A Troublesome Toy," cover illustration for Life magazine, 1911.

Advertisement for Oneida Community Silver. Collection of the Society of Illustrators Museum of American Illustration.

"Senorita with Silverware." Photo courtesy of the Archives of the American Illustrators Gallery, New York City.

"There is a Santa Claus," cover illustration for Life magazine, December 1926. Photo courtesy of the Archives of the American Illustrators Gallery, New York City.

Illustration for Holeproof Hosiery advertisement. The Charles Martignette Collection.

"Elephant Offering to Egyptian Woman," illustration for Fiberloid Corporation advertisement, 1922. Photo courtesy of the Archives of the American Illustrators Gallery, New York City.

Illustration for Watkins Mulsified Cocoanut Oil for Shampooing, 1917. Photo courtesy of the Archives of the American Illustrators Gallery, New York City.

"Our New Silverware," illustration for Oneida Community Silver advertisement in The Saturday Evening Post, *November 22, 1913. Photo courtesy of the Archives of the American Illustrators Gallery, New York City.*

"Wedding Gift." Photo courtesy of the Archives of the American Illustrators Gallery, New York City.

Cover illustration for Good Housekeeping, *January 1915. Photo courtesy of Illustration House, Inc.*

Born and raised in Chicago, Harry Anderson attended the University of Illinois thinking he would pursue a career in mathematics. He soon discovered, however, that the path he wanted to follow was that of an artist. This interest in painting led him to enroll at Syracuse University in 1927. There he met and became fast friends with Tom Lovell. Graduating at the depth of the Depression, the two aspiring artists set up a studio in New York's Greenwich Village and together struggled through that difficult period.

By 1934, Anderson was getting regular assignments for editorial work, but he was not happy in New York and moved back to Chicago, where he joined the Stevens-Gross art agency. There he specialized mainly in advertising illustration, later joining up with Haddon Sundblom's group. In the 1940s Anderson began illustrating for the *Review* and Herald Publishing Association, which is affiliated with the Seventh Day Adventist Church. His depiction of religious themes comprised about half of his output and in 1946 prompted a move to Washington, D.C. in order to be near the publisher's headquarters. Within five years, however, Anderson felt the need to be near an illustration community, which Washington did not have, and moved to Connecticut where many successful illustrators lived.

Anderson believed that conception, composition, values, colors and painting dexterity must all work together—and that they are important in just that order. It was his mastery of those elements that led to his success, plus the fact that his characters were real people that the public could identify with.

Because of an allergy to oil paint, Anderson became a watercolorist, using tube opaque watercolors whose properties most resemble the qualities of oils. For more than 60 years his work appeared in scores of advertisements such as Coca-Cola, Cream of Wheat, General Electric, and magazines such as *The Saturday Evening Post, Cosmopolitan, McCall's* and *Redbook*.

"The Graduate," illustration for Massachusetts Mutual Life Insurance Co. advertisement, 1983. Collection of the Society of Illustrators Museum of American Illustration.

"Round Trip," illustration for The Ladies' Home Journal, *April 1949. Collection of the Society of Illustrators Museum of American Illustration.*

Collection of the Society of Illustrators Museum of American Illustration.

ELIZABETH SHIPPEN GREEN

(1 8 7 1 - 1 9 5 4)

At an early age, Elizabeth Shippen Green's fascination with the illustrations she saw in children's books instilled in her the desire to study art. Encouraged by her father, an amateur artist, she began drawing flowers when she was a child. Later, Howard Pyle's drawings in *St. Nicholas* inspired her to become an illustrator.

Born in Philadelphia, Green enrolled at the Pennsylvania Academy of the Fine Arts when she was 18. At the same time, she began drawing women's fashions for department store catalogues and newspapers, and occasionally sent drawings to children's magazines.

In 1896 she enrolled in Howard Pyle's illustration classes at Drexel Institute, where she met and became lifelong friends with Jessie Willcox Smith and Violet Oakley. She collaborated with Smith on *The Book of the Child*, which brought them wide popularity.

Green credited Pyle with teaching her "how to interpret life." Under his tutelage she gained the skills necessary to move from being an advertising artist to a short story illustrator. Commissions came from leading magazines of the day—*The Saturday Evening Post*, *St. Nicholas*, *Woman's Home Companion* and *The Ladies' Home Journal*. An exclusive contract with *Harper's Monthly* guaranteed that her charming drawings would grace the magazine's pages from 1901 to the mid–1920s.

Occasionally she accepted lucrative advertising assignments for Kodak , Ivory soap, Elgin watches and Peerless ice cream freezers.

Her illustration, "The Thousand Quilt," shows her very brilliant use of color and decorative skills. By outlining the important elements in her illustrations her work became more forceful and greatly enhanced the reproduction of her work, whether in black-and-white or in color.

In 1911 Green married Huger Elliott, an architect and lecturer. They moved to Rhode Island where he became director of the Rhode Island School of Design. They collaborated on a book of illustrated nonsense verses and eventually retired to Philadelphia.

"Watching the Clouds Go By." Photo courtesy of Illustration House, Inc.

"Masquerade," illustration for Harper's Monthly, *July 1909. Collection of Alan Goffman.*

"The Thousand Quilt," *illustration for* Harper's Monthly, *December 1904. Photo courtesy of the Archives of the American Illustrators Gallery, New York City.*

Architecture and the human figure were the main focal points of Ben Shahn's art. He was noted for his striking drawings on the covers of jazz and classical record albums. In his illustration for "Jazz," opposite, a minimum of bold, graphic lines quickly characterize the musician. Whereas he captured the essence of figures with a limited number of brush strokes, his stylized, intricate renderings of buildings were drawn in minute detail, with each brick, stone and piece of wood in place.

Shahn was a muralist as well, and illustrated numerous books by major authors. At times he hand lettered the text, sometimes on rare paper, and often he would bind a book by hand. Among his advertising clients were many "Fortune 500" companies, and over the years his work appeared in magazines such as *Fortune, Time, Look, The Nation, Charm, Seventeen, Esquire* and *Scientific American.*

Shahn was born in Lithuania and emigrated to New York in 1906. After attending New York University, City College and the National Academy of Design, he traveled for a time in Europe and North Africa. During the Depression his poster designs were much in demand for government relief programs, and with the advent of World War II he created posters for the Office of War Information. After the war, Shahn's stylized illustrations expressed the anxiety and solitude of modern urban life.

One of the first magazine illustration assignments he accepted came from *Harper's* and concerned a tragic coal mine disaster in Illinois. Shahn overwhelmed the editor by appearing at his office at the appointed hour with 60 drawings. *Harper's* had room for only 20 or so, but subsequently published a brochure containing the whole group. The drawings alone did not satisfy Shahn's concern over the disaster and its ramifications. He followed them with three paintings: "Mine Disaster," now in the Metropolitan Museum of Art, "Death of a Miner" and "Miner's Wives," now owned by the Museum of Modern Art.

Illustration for the film "Ambassador Satchmo," 1956. Private collection.

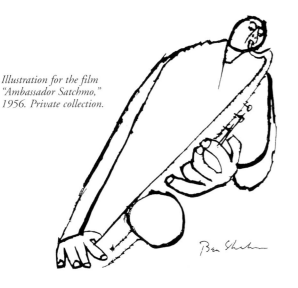

Illustration for the film "Ambassador Satchmo," 1956. Private collection.

Illustration for the film "Ambassador Satchmo," 1956. Private collection.

"Jazz," c. 1966. Photo courtesy of the Archives of the American Illustrators Gallery, New York City.

(b .   1 9 1 2)

In the late 1940s "pulp fiction" was coined in the publishing trade as the definition of a new kind of book—the paperback novel. James Avati was responsible for heralding in that new genre of illustration and became known as "the king" of paperback illustration. He was the first artist to make memorable images on the covers of paperback editions of contemporary American writing.

Avati lived most of his life in Red Bank, New Jersey, where his father had been a professional photographer. He attended Mercersburg Academy and Princeton University, where he earned a B.A. in architecture. Entering the job market in the middle of the 1930s Depression, he found a little work in ad agencies and as a decorative painter for a New York department store. In 1942 he joined the Army, served in the European theater, and upon his discharge returned to art school with the help of the GI bill.

In 1948 New American Library hired Avati to illustrate some of their paperback covers. His artwork sold a lot of books and was largely responsible for the tremendous success of paperbacks. In due time Avati worked for every publisher of paperback books. His realistic style suited the earthy novels of the best contemporary writers, among them William Faulkner, Pearl Buck, William Styron, Irwin Shaw and Erskine Caldwell.

His illustrations picked up the gritty realism of American life as recorded by these novelists.

In the painting opposite, Avati sets the stage for *Lie Down in Darkness* with a subdued palette punctuated with accents of bright color. Placed in the intimacy of a small room, with clothing and furnishings in disarray, his characters act out a story about to unfold. Avati's use of everyday locations, props, and neighborhood people as models, added to the down-to-earth realism of his illustrations.

At the age of 75, after two marriages and nine children, he moved to Petaluma, California, to pursue yet another romance and to fulfill his lifelong dream of applying his skills to fine art.

Photo courtesy of the Society of Illustrators Archives.

My Three Daughters, *illustration for Simon & Schuster, 1978. Photo courtesy of the Society of Illustrators Archives.*

Cover illustration for Goodbye to Berlin, *for Signet Paperback Books, May 1952. The Charles Martignette Collection.*

Illustration for Lie Down in Darkness. *Photo courtesy of Illustration House, Inc.*

Although McClelland Barclay is best known for his illustrations of beautiful women, his first paintings were of the sea. His early years as a sailor and fisherman instilled in him a passion for the sea that permeated his whole life. He joined the Navy during World War I and in 1940 returned to active duty in the Pacific as a Lieutenant Commander.

Barclay grew up in St. Louis, Missouri, attended the St. Louis Museum of Fine Arts, then the Art Institute of Chicago, the Corcoran Museum in Washington D.C. and the Art Students League. He studied under H.C. Ives, George Bridgman and Thomas Fogarty.

Barclay's painting on the facing page, which focuses on a lean, athletic woman, reflects the influence of his early training in Bridgman's anatomy class. Although painted years ago, this woman seems timeless—except for the change in swimsuit fashions she could be the most recent supermodel. Bold, sunny colors give her the appearance of glowing good health. Here Barclay has combined his two loves—painting the sea and a beautiful woman.

During the 1920s and '30s he painted a series of sophisticated and stylishly dressed women for the General Motors "Body by Fisher" advertising campaign which became a huge success and brought him much deserved recognition. He worked for magazines such as *The Ladies' Home Journal*, *Cosmopolitan*, *The Saturday Evening Post* and *Redbook*, illustrating the short stories of Faith Baldwin, Louis Bromfield and other noted authors. But "pretty girls" were not all he painted. Some of his advertising clients included Texaco, Mobil Oil, Whitman's Chocolates, Camel and Chesterfield cigarettes.

Aside from advertising and editorial assignments, over the years Barclay produced many recruitment posters for the war effort and for the Red Cross, and painted portraits of Naval officers. He also painted a portrait of General Douglas MacArthur while they were in the South Pacific.

In July 1943 Barclay was reported missing in action on a torpedoed LST in the Solomon Sea, two weeks before he was scheduled to return home.

"Action at Sea." Collection of the Society of Illustrators Museum of American Illustration.

Cover illustration. The Charles Martignette Collection.

Advertisement for Coca-Cola. The Charles Martignette Collection.

"Waterskiing," cover illustration for Country Gentleman, *August 1940. Photo courtesy of Illustration House, Inc. © 1940 by The Curtis Publishing Company.*

JOSEPH CLEMENT COLL

(1 8 8 1 - 1 9 2 1)

Revered as one of America's greatest pen-and-ink renderers, Joseph Clement Coll used his penpoint like a brush—subtly, with fine lines, as well as boldly, with strong slashes of black. His ingenious use of white areas helped create a full spectrum of values in his pictures. He was a fine colorist and an accomplished painter as well.

Early in life Coll decided to pursue a career in art. At the age of 15 he took a job as an apprentice in the art department of the *New York American*, a Hearst newspaper. He worked his way up from drawing borders and spots to inking portraits over silver prints, then on to reportorial assignments. After this basic training he was sent to the *Chicago American*, and eventually the newly-formed *North American* in Philadelphia hired him. Since printing techniques were limited at the time, his pen-and-ink sketches were perfect for newspaper reproduction.

In later years, his work appeared in *Harper's Bazaar*, *Redbook*, *Cosmopolitan* and *The Ladies' Home Journal*. His remarkable imagination, combined with his technical skill, made him the ideal person to illustrate stories by Arthur Conan Doyle and the long series of Fu Manchu adventures in *Collier's Weekly*.

Coll's illustration on the facing page, depicting an elegant woman enjoying a ride in the park, is typical of his great tonal control through size, shape, density and direction of pen strokes. The Spanish master, Daniel Vierge, was Coll's idol and inspiration. Vierge's dazzling variety of pen strokes and use of solid blacks led Coll to successfully emulate his style. Others who influenced Coll were Edwin Austin Abbey and Howard Pyle.

Coll illustrated several books and his work appeared in many periodicals until his sudden death from appendicitis at the age of forty.

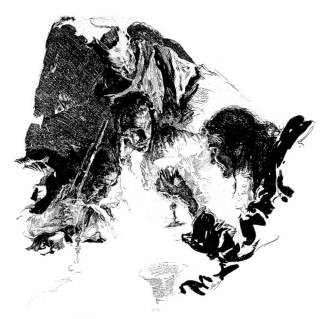

Photo courtesy of Illustration House, Inc.

"For the Man That's Well Fed Sirs, Can Never Do Ill." Photo courtesy of Illustration House, Inc.

"Ladies and Gents." Collection of the Society of Illustrators Museum of American Illustration.

"Peggy in the Park," illustration for the Associated Sunday Magazine. *Collection of the Society of Illustrators Museum of American Illustration.*

F R A N K S C H O O N O V E R

(1 8 7 7 - 1 9 7 2)

An advertisement in the *Philadelphia Inquirer* for Howard Pyle's composition class at Drexel Institute changed Frank Earle Schoonover's career goal from the ministry to art. He enrolled in 1896 and became one of the ten selected for Pyle's coveted summer class at Chadds Ford. Schoonover was thrilled four years later when Pyle handed him a manuscript to illustrate—his first commercial assignment.

During the next 40 years Schoonover turned out over 2500 illustrations, numbered each one, notated the date, article, publisher, medium, size and models. Even costs were faithfully recorded in his daybook.

His covers for *Robin Hood, Treasure Island, Kidnapped*, and many other books published by *Harper's* were enjoyed by a whole generation of children. Dozens of books about cowboys, pirates, presidents, folk heroes and Knights of the Round Table were filled with his illustrations. The demand for his work increased greatly as the market for adventure and western frontier literature grew.

In the Breakfast Cocoa advertisement on the facing page he created a scene which vividly reflects his thorough knowledge of outdoor life. All the elements give the viewer a real sense of the campsite. Particularly interesting is how he achieved the hazy effect of smoke with dabs of dappled blue-gray paint. His well-designed composition and the boldness with which he applied paint combine to make it a very successful picture.

An assignment in 1903 led him to the Hudson Bay region for background research and served to make him an expert on the Objibwa tribe who made him a blood brother and named him "Misanagan," or picture-making man.

Schoonover did a series of World War I paintings for *The Ladies' Home Journal* which hang in the Delaware State Armory, and a church boasts 13 magnificent stained glass windows based on his illustrations.

Schoonover's transition from illustrator to easel painter in 1941 resulted in approximately 200 paintings of the Brandywine and Delaware River valleys. His studios in Wilmington, Delaware, now restored and open to the public, serve as a museum and conservation gallery.

Photo courtesy of Schoonover Studios Ltd.

"Trapper with Christmas Tree." Photo courtesy of Schoonover Studios Ltd.

Photo courtesy of Schoonover Studios Ltd.

"More Sustaining Power for Hunters, Tourists and Students," advertisement for Walter Baker & Co. Breakfast Cocoa, 1905 Hudson Bay Expedition. The Charles Martignette Collection.

"Racing to the Fire."
Photo courtesy of
Schoonover Studios Ltd.

Photo courtesy of Illustration House, Inc.

"Rustlers of Silver River," illustration for Country Gentleman, *December 1929. Photo courtesy of Illustration House, Inc.*

Photo courtesy of Schoonover Studios Ltd.

Herbert Tauss's work has been one of constant reinvention, evolving on every level. His vision goes beyond purely technical skills and his sensitive line is a virtual reflection of his feelings. Whether in black-and-white or color, his work has the ability to pique the curiosity of the viewer. One is compelled to learn what lies behind the intriguing image of the beautiful woman on the facing page. The depth of emotion Tauss expresses in this painting is appreciated when one discovers that it is a portrait of his beloved late wife.

Tauss's early years in New York were typical of a first generation immigrant family's life—survival being the code word. Although his world was insulated, cramped and colorless, he somehow developed an interest in art while still in his teens. After graduating from the High School of Industrial Arts, he was hired as an apprentice in a studio for $18 a week. Eventually he joined Charles E. Cooper Studio where Coby Whitmore, whose illustrations Tauss had always admired, took an interest in him and was instrumental in getting him an assignment from *McCall's* magazine—his first double-page spread.

After doing some work for British women's magazines, Tauss extended his trip abroad and traveled through Europe with his family. Though he returned nearly broke, it turned out to be an invaluable and enriching learning experience. In the ensuing 30 years he drew, sculpted and painted for numerous major magazines including *The Saturday Evening Post*, *Redbook*, *Good Housekeeping*, *Pageant*, *American Weekly* and *Parents*.

In the mid-1970s Tauss began illustrating classics for The Franklin Library, and in 1982 he created illustrations for a collection of stories by Isaac Bashevis Singer. Aiming for a "biblical look," he drew with charcoal on canvas for the first time, a medium he grew to love.

Tauss has received numerous awards from the Art Directors Club, the Society of Illustrators and Communication Arts, and his work is in government and private collections.

"Mr. Malloy," illustration for the Franklin Library edition of Cannery Row.
Collection of the Society of Illustrators Museum of American Illustration.

"Simon Bolivar," illustration for The Battle of Junin, for the National Geographic Society. Collection of the artist.

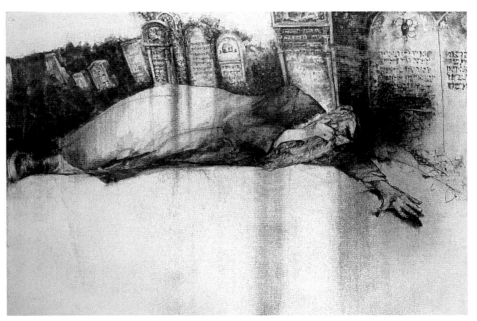

"Gimpel the Fool," illustration for The Franklin Library. Collection of the artist.

"Joan Tauss," portrait of the artist's wife. Collection of the artist.

The authenticity with which Anton Otto Fischer painted ships and nautical scenes stemmed from first-hand experience gained during his years at sea. Born in Germany and orphaned at an early age, Fischer was sent to live with an uncle who reluctantly took him in. At 16, he was working for a printer when he saw something that fired his imagination—a travel poster of a ship under full sail. Seeking an escape to his unhappy life, he ran away and spent eight years on a variety of sailing ships.

While on a layover in New York, he decided to stay, applied for American citizenship and got a job as model and handyman for illustrator A.B. Frost. Recognizing Fischer's artistic talent, Frost encouraged him to go to Paris, where he studied for two years at the Academie Julian under Jean Paul Laurens.

After his return to America in 1908 he sold his first illustration to *Harper's Weekly*. There followed commissions from *Everybody's* magazine to illustrate stories by Jack London, and in 1910 he began a 48-year association with *The Saturday Evening Post*. By the 1930s, Fischer was known for his excellent painting skills and his knowledge of sailing.

His rendering of the Gwydyr Castle, opposite, was a labor of love—it was a vessel with which he had been personally involved. His palette is fairly muted, but nevertheless shows a full range of color. There appears to be a horizontal division of color—the warm range above, cool colors below. It's a splendid example of his mastery of marine painting. In 1947 Fischer wrote and illustrated *Fo'c'sle Days*, a book about the rigors and adventures of his earliest years at sea.

During World War II, the U.S. Coast Guard conferred the rank of Lieutenant Commander on him as "Artist Laureate." Upon returning from North Atlantic convoy duty, he painted a stirring series of paintings which appeared in *Life* magazine and were exhibited at the Corcoran Gallery in Washington, D.C.

"The Pequod Becalmed."

"Longshoremen," book illustration, c. 1950. Photo courtesy of Illustration House, Inc.

"Moby Dick."

"Tugboat Annie," illustration for The Saturday Evening Post, *1935. Collection of the Society of Illustrators Museum of American Illustration.*

Story illustration, 1924. Photo courtesy of Illustration House, Inc.

"The Gwydyr Castle," Photo courtesy of Illustration House, Inc.

Over a dozen members of Violet Oakley's family were professional artists. She once described her desire to paint as hereditary and chronic, and stated that she was born with a paint-brush in her mouth instead of a silver spoon.

She attended the Art Students League for a year, then left for Paris to study at the Academie Montparnasse. Later she went to England and studied with Charles Lasar, an artist whose emphasis on decorative design had a lasting effect on her work. As seen in her sketch for the cover of *Country Life* below, the intricate border framing the picture plays a dominant role in the composition.

Upon her return to America in 1896, she enrolled in the Pennsylvania Academy of the Fine Arts, then switched to the Drexel Institute to study with Howard Pyle. By using a combination of watercolor, crayon and ink, Oakley developed her own unique style. She applied crayon broadly to textured paper, creating patterns of light and dark, and drew outlines around the figures, separating each from the background. Because of her strong color sense and compositional skill, Pyle encouraged her to start working in a larger, more decorative style. That was the beginning of her long career as a designer of stained glass windows and murals.

In 1902, after completing murals and stained glass windows for the All Angels Church in New York, she received her largest commission—to decorate the Governor's Reception Room at the new Pennsylvania State Capitol. Edwin Austin Abbey was painting another portion of the murals, and when he died, Oakley completed that as well, taking nineteen years to finish the nine murals.

For many years Oakley shared studios and homes with Elizabeth Shippen Green and Jessie Willcox Smith, fellow students at Drexel with whom she had developed lifelong friendships. Oakley won many awards and in 1948 received an honorary degree of Doctor of Laws from the Drexel Institute.

"Henry VIII and Anne Boleyn." Photo courtesy of Illustration House, Inc.

"Forget Also Thine Own People and Thy Father's House," study for a mural of Admiral Sir William Penn denouncing and turning his son from home, c. 1903. Collection of the Brandywine River Museum, Museum Volunteers' Purchase Fund, 1978.

Cover illustration for Country Life. *The Charles Martignette Collection.*

Lenten cover for Collier's Weekly, *1899. Collection of Mr. and Mrs. Benjamin Eisenstat.*

The "mood" that Mead Schaeffer strove for, he said, came out of a psyche more akin to that of a writer than a painter, which would explain the strong narrative thread in his paintings. His work divided itself into two periods: the early one dealt with romantic, swashbuckling and theatrical subjects; the second was more reportorial, based on authentic, factual themes.

One of his earlier paintings appears on the facing page. The fact that it is only a two-color illustration does not diminish its power—it still reflects his strong sense of design and bold approach in applying paint to canvas. Schaeffer believed, as did Harvey Dunn, that it was important to have brush strokes clearly visible in order to give it a more painterly quality.

Born in Freedom Plains, New York, Schaeffer decided what he wanted to be when, at age seven, he got a whiff of turpentine in an artist's studio. He attended Pratt Institute, then studied with Dean Cornwell and Harvey Dunn. Their influence is reflected in Schaeffer's strong compositions and powerfully executed paintings.

Schaeffer was illustrating for the major magazines while still in his twenties. He also illustrated a series of 16 classics, including *The Count of Monte Cristo*, *Les Miserables* and *Moby Dick*. Eventually he became dissatisfied with romance and costume stories and wanted to deal with contemporary subjects. *The Saturday Evening Post* was featuring Americana at the time and artists were traveling to different parts of the country to find material with national appeal. Schaeffer and Norman Rockwell, neighbors in Vermont, went on an extended trip to the West which resulted in many fine covers for the *Post*.

During World War II, Schaeffer created a pictorial chronicle of the 14 branches of the Armed Services for the *Post* which were exhibited in over 90 cities.

Although Schaeffer had suffered a stroke, in 1980 he made a valiant effort to attend a luncheon of old friends at the Society of Illustrators where he collapsed and died among his fellow illustrators.

"Molly Brant," illustration for Women America Remembers. *Collection of the Society of Illustrators Museum of American Illustration.*

"The Bishop and the Beggar, illustration for The Saturday Evening Post, *1944. Collection of Mr. and Mrs. Gerald McConnell.*

"The Blue Roadster," illustration for American *magazine. Collection of the Society of Illustrators Museum of American Illustration.*

"The Forbidden Lovers," illustration for The Ladies' Home Journal, *July 1932. The Charles Martignette Collection.*

(1 8 6 7 - 1 9 3 4)

Most of Winsor McCay's comic strips revolved around dreams, fantasies and nightmares. His "Little Nemo in Slumberland" was a Sunday feature filled with fantastical worlds in gorgeous color, detailed drawings and Art Nouveau-flavored decorations. His pen-and-ink style, with its heavy outlining of figures and use of bold color, was copied by art deco and poster artists of the time.

On the facing page is a full-color strip which shows McCay's imagination at its best. His draftsmanship is flawless, as is his dialogue. While merely looking at his work tickles the viewer, by reading the story one can partake of the fun McCay must have had in creating these strips.

McCay was raised in Spring Lake, Michigan, and worked as a vaudeville performer where he dazzled audiences with lightning-quick chalk talks and caricatures which he sold for a quarter.

In 1889 he got a job with a printing company in Chicago, then moved to the *Cincinnati Commercial Tribune* in 1891, where his comic strip career began. Two years later he went to work for the *Cincinnati Enquirer* and free-lanced for *Life*, the cartoon weekly.

Although McCay created other strips, Nemo was the most successful. There was a book of Little Nemo adventures, a Broadway operetta, postcards, playing cards and games. The strip ran from 1905 to 1911—until McCay went to work for Hearst, where he drew powerful editorial cartoons and a strip called "In the Land of Wonderful Dreams."

McCay helped to develop animated film and deserves great credit for pioneering the art of frame-by-frame animation. "Little Nemo" was released in 1911, followed by others, including "Gertie the Dinosaur" and "How the Mosquito Operates."

As wild and glamorous as Little Nemo was, its creator was anything but. A modest fellow, he worked quietly right up to the day he died, his half-finished editorial cartoon published the day after his death.

"Is My Lid on Straight?" political cartoon of Father Knickerbocker and the Tammany Tiger. Collection of Mr. and Mrs. Gerald McConnell.

"Thank Heaven for Progress." Collection of the Society of Illustrators Museum of American Illustration.

"Flying Carpet Above Road Rally," 1910. Collection of the Society of Illustrators Museum of American Illustration.

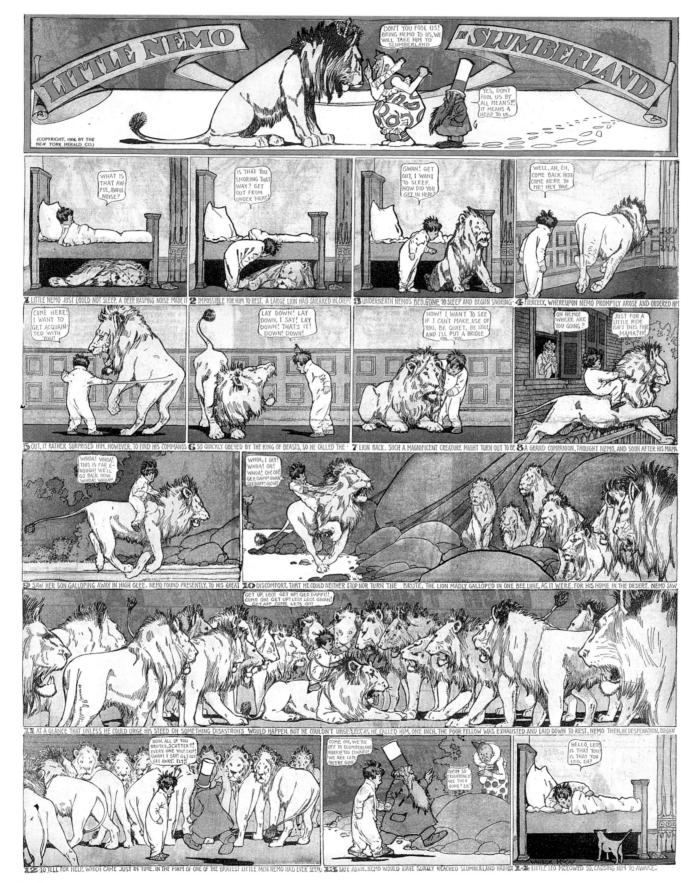

"Little Nemo," from The Complete Collection of Little Nemo in Slumberland *for Slumberland Productions.*

A woodcut executed by Richard Mather in 1670 is the first example of what came to be known as American illustration, but it wasn't until three hundred years later that a full-fledged market for illustration was created. In 1975, Walt Reed began selling vintage illustration to the general public, and a year later the Society of Illustrators sponsored the 200 Years of American Illustration exhibition at the New-York Historical Society. A book documenting that historic event was then published by Edward Booth Clibborn. The publication of Walt and Roger Reed's book, *The Illustrator in America 1880–1980*, further enlightened the public of this art form. By the early 1980s there was enough public interest to support a series of auctions of illustration at several New York galleries. Various television specials and short films also helped promote the art of illustration, and hundreds of new collectors from varied backgrounds and professions entered the arena.

Illustrators themselves were the first collectors of American illustration. In 1979, a Massachusetts contractor was renovating the former residence of Charles Sheldon when he discovered a 'secret' room filled with original works by artists such as J.C. Leyendecker, Howard Chandler Christy, Maxfield Parrish and Charles Dana Gibson. Sheldon, creator of the Breck Girl Shampoo ads, also painted portraits of movie stars of the 1920s and '30s for the front covers of Hollywood fan magazines. Letters between Sheldon and other artists revealed that trading of each other's artwork was going on.

For years illustrators have been viewed as less than "fine artists" by a vast majority of collectors and museums. The time has come for art historians and collectors alike to give illustrators and their work proper recognition. Today's enthusiastic collectors of illustration will continue to influence how this art is viewed, and the Society of Illustrators Museum of American Illustration will continue to lead the way in order to achieve that goal. The 21st century is destined to document the true importance of America's illustrators and their invaluable contributions to American history and cultural heritage.

KATHERINE HEPBURN

DOLORES DEL RIO

SHIRLEY TEMPLE

MYRNA LOY

CLARA BOW

Pastel portraits by Charles Gates Sheldon. The Charles Martignette Collection.

THE WORLD'S LARGEST COLLECTION
AMERICAN ILLUSTRATION ART
ORIGINAL, PAINTINGS, PASTELS, WATERCOLORS, DRAWINGS

Individually priced for sale to qualified buyers are **THOUSANDS** of diversified subject and choice images. Executed between 1890 and 1990 these illustrations were published and reproduced as America's **Magazine Front Cover Art, Magazine Story Illustrations, Paperback Novel Cover Art, Advertising Art, Calendar Art, Pulp Art, Children's Book Art, Glamour & Pin-Up Art.**

J.C. LEYENDECKER,
(1874–1951) "Record Time-Cool Summer Comfort" Oil on Canvas, 22 x 21, Unsigned. Country Gentleman's Magazine inside front cover, June 12, 1920. Kuppenheimer Men's Clothing Advertisement.

J.C. LEYENDECKER,
(1874–1951) "The Little Thief" Oil on Canvas, 30 x 21, Signed, Lower Right, Saturday Evening Post front cover, August 7, 1915.

HARRISON FISHER,
(1875–1934) "Dear Sweetheart" Watercolor on Illustration Board, 28 x 20, Signed, Lower Left, American Sunday Monthly Magazine front cover, May 3, 1914.

ALBERTO VARGAS,
(1896–1984) "Glorifying The American Girl" Watercolor on Illustration Board, 17 x 12, Signed, Lower Right. Paramount Pictures Corp. Advertisement & Movie Poster Art, 1927.

ALBERTO VARGAS,
(1896–1984) "Robe Du Apres-Midi" Watercolor on heavy paper, 29 x 22, Signed & Dated, Lower Left, 1932. Fashion Illustration after a Vogue Magazine cover. Reproduced as a full page in the famous book, VARGAS (Crown Publishing Co. 1978).

GIL ELVGREN, (1914–1980) "From The Bottom Up—A Weighty Problem" Oil on Canvas, 30 x 24, Signed, Lower Right. Published in 1962. Brown & Bigelow Calendars, Ink Blotters, Note Pads, and Playing Card Decks.

A PRIVATE GALLERY LOCATED IN THE MIAMI–FORT LAUDERDALE METROPOLITAN REGION IS OPEN BY APPOINTMENT.

MEAD SCHAEFFER,
(1898–1980) "The Summertime Swimming Hole" Oil on Illustration Board, 22 x 17, Signed, Lower Left. Saturday Evening Post, front cover, June 25, 1949.

PAUL BRANSOM,
(1885–1979) "A Vision of Beauty" Watercolor & Charcoal on Illustration Board, 24 x 18.5, Signed, Lower Right. Country Gentlemen Magazine, front cover, October 1930.

GEORGE HUGHES, (b. 1907) "Little Brother Listens In" Oil on Masonite Board, 22 x 21, Signed, Lower Left. Saturday Evening Post, front cover, October 10, 1956.

CHARLES G. MARTIGNETTE
P.O. BOX 293, Hallandale, Florida 33008 USA Telephone: (954) 454-3474

Bank and trade references are required.

To the collector, a hall of fame is a personal

Coles Phillips
gouache and watercolor

Dean Cornwell
conté pencil

Frederick Remington
watercolor en grisaille and graphite

Norman Rockwell
oil on board

Theodore S. Geisel "Dr. Seuss"
charcoal and watercolor en grisaille

Maxfield Parrish
oil on stretched paper

James Montgomery Flagg
watercolor

concept. Let us help you realize yours.

George Petty *watercolor*

Walter Biggs
oil on canvas

J. C. Leyendecker *oil on canvas*

N. C. Wyeth
oil on canvas

George Herriman *ink & watercolor*

Reynold Brown
gouache & lettering

Howard Pyle
oil on canvas

217

THE WORLD'S LARGEST COLLECTION
AMERICAN PIN-UP & GLAMOUR ART
ORIGINAL PAINTINGS, PASTELS, WATERCOLORS, DRAWINGS

Individually priced for sale to qualified buyers are <u>several hundred</u> rare original Pin-Up & Glamour Art Paintings. Executed between 1920 and 1980, these famous images were published and reproduced as Calendar Art Illustrations, Magazine Front Covers, Magazine Centerfolds, and Advertising Specialty Products.

All major and important artists are available:

ALBERTO VARGAS	GEORGE PETTY	GIL ELVGREN
Patrick Nagel	Robert Blue	Earl Moran
Rolf Armstrong	Billy DeVorss	Art Frahm
Zoe Mozert	Joyce Ballantyne	Pearl Frush
Peter Driben	Edward Runci	Arthur Sarnoff
Fritz Willis	Jules Erbit	K.O. Munson
Enoch Bolles	Cardwell S. Higgins	Charles Sheldon
Al Buell	T.N. Thompson	Bradshaw Crandell
Walt Otto	D'Ancona	Bill Ward
Mabel Rollins Harris	Gene Pressler	Carl Shreve
Harry Ekman	Medcalf	Earl MacPherson

GIL ELVGREN, "Teacher's Pet", Oil On Canvas, 30 x 24, Signed, Lower Right. Published, 1968, Brown & Bieglow Calendar.

GEORGE PETTY, "Summertime Delight", Watercolor, Gouache, Airbrush, 20 x 14, Signed Loewer Left. Published in Esquire Magazine, July, 1937. Also used as an ad by Jantzen Swim Suit Co. and reproduced in the famous Esquire Petty Phone Book, 1941

ALBERTO VARGAS, "Miss January, 1946" Watercolor and airbrush, 32 x 18. Published as unique four-page centerfold in Esquire Magazine, January ,1946

SPECIAL NOTICE
In addition to the Pin-Up & Glamour Art material, a vast inventory of "mainstream" American Illustration Art is also for sale.
<u>Several thousand</u> original paintings by America's top 100 illustators (circa, 1890-1990) are available including:

Howard Pyle	Norman Rockwell	J.C. Leyendecker
Charles Dana Gibson	Harrison Fisher	James Montgomery Flagg
Dean Cornwell	Jessie Wilcox Smith	Mead Schaffer
John Falter	Stevan Dohanas	Amos Sewell

A PRIVATE GALLERY LOCATED IN THE FORT LAUDERDALE-MIAMI
AREA IS NOW OPEN BY APPOINTMENT
Bank and trade references are required. Please call after 2 PM EST.

CHARLES G. MARTIGNETTE
P.O. BOX 293, Hallandale, Florida 33008 USA Telephone: (954) 454-3474

Author of <u>The Great American Pin-up</u> published worldwide by Benedikt Taschen Verlag, October 1996.

"The great band of illustrators — Howard Pyle, A.B., Frost, Maxfield Parrish, Edwin Austin Abbey, Charles Dana Gibson and many, many more — have shown us to ourselves. I am proud and happy to have been one of their company."
— Norman Rockwell

The Norman Rockwell Museum at Stockbridge salutes the men and women of the great band of Hall of Fame illustrators, past, present and future.

The museum holds the world's largest collection of Norman Rockwell artwork, the illustrator's archives and his studio. The museum presents exhibitions and programs featuring the art of visual communication and is open year-round, except New Year's Day, Thanksgiving and Christmas.

The
**Norman
Rockwell
Museum**
at Stockbridge

P.O. Box 308, Stockbridge, MA 01262
413-298-4100   www.NRM.org

THE CREAM OF WHEAT COLLECTION

N. C. Wyeth
(1882-1945)
*"Where The
Mail Goes
Cream of
Wheat Goes"*
1908

Charles Leslie
Thrasher
(1889-1936)
"Playing Hooky"
1912

Created during the "Golden Age of Illustration"...
Stored, by chance, in an archivally sound environment...
And rescued from obscurity by a diligent archivist...

The Cream of Wheat Collection of over 1600 original
works of advertising art is a unique player in illustration
history that has toured the nation.

Harry Anderson	Mac Martin
Stanley M. Arthurs	Helen Mason
H. S. Benton	Frederick Kimball Mizen
E. B. Bird	Galen G. Perrett
Helen Blackburn	John Rae
M. L. Blumenthal	Henry Patrick Raleigh
M. Leone Bracker	Fletcher Ransom
Worth Brehm	Otto Schneider
E. V. Brewer	John G. Scott
Mabel Buckmaster	Jessie Willcox Smith
William V. Cahill	Rowland M. Smith
Charles Champe	Roy Frederic Spreter
Walter Appleton Clark	Alice Barber Stephens
Osgood Cochi	James Reeve Stuart
Arthur Crisp	Haddon Hubbard Sundblom
Maud Tousey Fangel	Leslie Thrasher
Denman Fink	Frank Verbeck
James Montgomery Flagg	Leslie Wallace
Alan Foster	Ernest Watson
Philip R Goodwin	Walter Whitehead
Norman T. Hall	C. G. Widney
Edwin Henry	Robert Wildhack
Frank B. Hoffman	Harry F. Wireman
John Newton Howitt	Katherine Richardson Wireman
August W. Hutaf	Newell Convers Wyeth
Henry Hutt	Florence Wyman
B. Corey Kilvert	
Harry B. Lachman	
Loyd L. LaDriere	
J. C. Leyendecker	
Andrew Loomis	
Philip Lyford	

NABISCO, INC.

7 Campus Drive
Parsippany, NJ 07862
Attn: Dave Stivers

airfloat
SYSTEMS, INC.

Innovative, Inexpensive, Reusable Packaging for Precious Artwork Like Yours

StrongBox®

Encase your fine, framed art in a protective environment. Three separate layers of foam protect your fine art fiom shock, plus optional "Puncture Guard" liners provide more protection than 3/8" plywood at a fraction of the weight. And, StrongBox is reusable. Eight sizes to meet your needs, all with Perf-Pack to custom fit your art.

PRINTPADS

Ship your prints flat in one of three sizes of PRINTPADs, our specially designed print shipping system which: you "customize" to fit your exact needs. Plus, it's reusable. Optional "Puncture Guard" Iiners add more urotection than 3/8" plywood with only 35% of the weight. The multi-layer design yields greatest possible protection.

GLASS SKIN

This moderately tacky glass covering helps prevent image damage to your painting or print surface resulting from accidental breakage during shipping. Glass Skin is inexpensive, removed instantly and leaves no residue.

> **AirFloat now custom designs boxes just for your specs and budget—they can be designed to any size!**
> **Coming soon Tri-Tubes and Stock Boxes from AirFloat!**

AIRFLOAT SYSTEMS
P.O. Box 229, Tupelo, MS 38802
National WATS (800) 445-2580* In Mississippi (601) 842-5219
FAX (800) 562-4323
Visit our web site at http://www.airfloatsys.com
E-mail: airfloat@airfloatsys.com

ALAN M. GOFFMAN
(1941 - 1997)

As an art dealer who specialized in illustrators such as Christy, Pyle, Rockwell, Leyendecker, and Parrish, he: "made contributions towards the recognition and acceptance of a fine group of artists who have been underrated and unappreciated for so long."

Howard Chandler Christy
"Americans All"
World War I recruiting poster, watercolor, collection of Alan M. Goffman

"The Dover Coach", 1935, Norman Rockwell

THE SOCIETY OF ILLUSTRATORS
MUSEUM OF AMERICAN ILLUSTRATION

exhibiting the best of contemporary and historic illustration. Tuesday - Saturday, year round, free admission.
The Society's Museum...Permanent Collection, Library, Archives and Museum Shop.

The Society of Illustrators was founded in 1901, incorporated as
a 50l (c) (3) not-for-profit educational organization in 1921
and established the Society of Illustrators Museum of
American Illustration in 1981.

128 East 63rd Street
New York, NY 10021-7392
(212) 838-2561 FAX
(800) SI MUSEUM (phone)
E-Mail: SI1901 @ aol.com

"Ladies Home Journal Cover", 1910
Harrison Fisher

"The Fadeaway Girl for Community Silverware", 1919,
Coles Phillips